APT AND
QUOT

Also available from Elliot Right Way Books

Sample Social Speeches
Wedding Speeches
Public Speaker's Joke Book
Right Joke For The Right Occasion

APT AND AMUSING QUOTATIONS

G. F. Lamb

RIGHT WAY

Printed and bound in Great Britain by Cox & Wyman Ltd., Reading, Berkshire.

The *Right Way* series is published by Elliot Right Way Books, Brighton Road, Lower Kingswood, Tadworth, Surrey, KT20 6TD, U.K. For information about our company and the other books we publish, visit our web site at www.right-way.co.uk

CONTENTS

INTRODUCTION

There are many kinds of humour, and this fact is reflected in the quotations I have gathered for this book. Some may make you smile or chuckle; a different sort will tickle your mind. Quotations have been drawn from a wide variety of sources. Many come from well-known humorists, but not all are comical. Some have been included because they offer an apt or pungent comment on a given topic. Deliberate nonsense will be found rubbing shoulders with unconscious absurdity.

This is not an academic treatise requiring precise details of source and date. However, as a matter of interest I have given the dates of authors born earlier than the eighteenth century. (But not Shakespeare's – anyone intelligent enough to be reading this book will know, without my having to tell him, that Shakespeare was an Elizabethan!) An author's title or other distinction is given only where there is a particular reason. For instance, it would be downright cruelty to deprive Byron of his rank; no one ever refers to him as George.

Apt and Amusing Quotations is designed partly to be useful to public speakers; a suitable quotation has often helped an after-dinner oration on its way. But the book is also intended for the general reader, who will, I hope, find it an agreeable field to browse in.

G.F.L.

Special note for public speakers

To speed research by topic, this book is arranged alphabetically under general subject headings. A complete list is to be found in the Contents. In addition, where possible, cross references to other sections that may be obviously or loosely connected, are given in the text beside each subject heading.

ABUSE– *see also* **ANGER, CRITICISM, CURSING, INSULTS.**
"You've never made anything or done anything that people can criticize. All they can really say about you is that you're a snob, a bigot, a racist, a chauvinist, an ignorant, insensitive, narrow-minded, intolerant, humourless wart."
ALAN AYCKBOURN

"Scum!" said the red-faced man. "Filthy, lousy, herring-gutted, spavin-bellied scum!" A. G. MACDONELL

"Thou art a boil,
A plague-sore, an embossed carbuncle!"
WILLIAM SHAKESPEARE *(King Lear)*

"He called me a muddle-headed old ass," he said. "Well, you are a muddle-headed old ass," I pointed out, quick as a flash.
P. G. WODEHOUSE

ACCIDENTS – *see also* **BOATS, HOSPITALS, MOTORING, RAILWAY, ROADS, TRAVEL.**

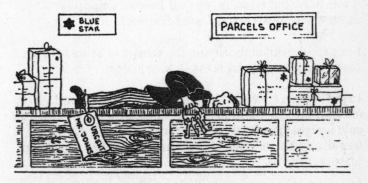

"There's been an accident," they said.
"Your servant's cut in half; he's dead!"
"Indeed!" said Mr Jones, "then please
Send me the half that's got my keys." HARRY GRAHAM

Once you start buying first-aid kits you start having accidents. GEORGE MIKES

"What is better than presence of mind in an accident?"
"Absence of body." *Punch*

ACTING – *see also* CINEMA, SHAKESPEARE, TELEVISION AND RADIO, THEATRE.
"Phoebe Lucas would play a glamorous courtesan with about as much sex appeal as a haddock!" NOEL COWARD

"He said that although he knew she was a formidable actress he'd rather have someone who looked less like a guinea-pig."
NOEL COWARD

They are a race apart, doomed to go through life pretending to be somebody else. R. F. DELDERFIELD

On the stage he was natural, simple, affecting;
'Twas only that when he was off he was acting.
OLIVER GOLDSMITH (on David Garrick)

I can speak with authority on the subject of being hard up. I have been a provincial actor. J. K. JEROME

In the first act I was cast for a snowball; in the second, an old man; in the third a smuggler; in the fourth, Man Friday. In case I might imagine that I was earning my salary too easily, I was also commandeered to play harlequin in the harlequinade.
EDMUND PAYNE

Actors like Shakespeare because they can gum on a lot of crêpe hair, bellow almost anything that comes into their heads, and then have their Lear taken seriously by the critics.
J. B. PRIESTLEY

I remember a landlady who used to split her dining-room into two halves: straight actors on the left, variety turns on the right. ERNIE WISE

ADULTERY – *see also* CHASTITY, HUSBANDS AND WIVES, LOVE, MARRIAGE, SEX.
Charles II does not appear to have practised birth control. In all he was to have thirteen illegitimate children.
MAURICE ASHLEY

Lament him, Mauchline husbands a',
  He often did assist ye;
For had ye staid whole weeks awa'
  Your wives they ne'er had missed ye.

Ye Mauchline bairns, as on ye pass,
  To school in bands together,
Oh, tread ye lightly on his grass,
  Perhaps he was your father. ROBERT BURNS

What men call gallantry, and gods adultery,
Is much more common when the climate's sultry.
LORD BYRON

Merely innocent flirtation,
Not quite adultery but adulteration. LORD BYRON

A little still she strove, and much repented,
And whispering, "I will ne'er consent" – consented.
LORD BYRON

Sarah could commit adultery at one end and weep for her sins at the other, and enjoy both operations at once. JOYCE CARY

Do not adultery commit
Advantage rarely comes of it. A. H. CLOUGH

"I love my neighbour as myself, and to avoid coveting my

neighbour's wife I desire to be coveted by her – which you know is another thing." WILLIAM CONGREVE (1670–1729)

Each deceiver to his cost may find
That marriage frauds too oft are paid in kind.
WILLIAM CONGREVE

"If the Husband be out of the way, the Wife may show her Fondness and Impatience of his Absence by choosing a lover as like him as she can." WILLIAM CONGREVE

Hypocrisy . . . cannot, like adultery or gluttony, be practised at spare moments. W. SOMERSET MAUGHAM

When Pontius wished an edict might be passed
That cuckolds should into the sea be cast,
His wife, assenting, thus replied to him:
"But first, my dear, I'd have you learn to swim."
MATTHEW PRIOR (1664–1721)

Simon Forman recognized that "illegitimate love" was immoral; but, like almost all humans, he kept his principles and his conduct in separate compartments. A. L. ROWSE

"Who would not make her husband a cuckold to make him a monarch?" WILLIAM SHAKESPEARE *(Othello)*

"No man worth having is true to his wife . . . or ever was." JOHN VANBRUGH (1664–1726)

ADVERTISING – *see also* HOUSE AND HOME.
There's a naive assumption that Saturday is the one day of the week when the halt and the maimed buy a paper. There are scores of advertisements for all-purpose back-rests, rupture appliances, step-in corselettes, wonder salts, and miracle bunion cures. DEREK COOPER

Wealth must be advertised, and the normal medium is obtrusively expensive goods. J. K. GALBRAITH

We all know nowadays that advertisement can be a fine art; but Nature made that discovery long ago, when bird-song burst into beauty. JULIAN HUXLEY

I never read a patent medicine advertisement without being impelled to the conclusion that I am suffering from the particular disease... in its most virulent form. J. K. JEROME

Advertising may be described as the science of arresting the human intelligence long enough to get money from it.
STEPHEN LEACOCK

Advertising is ... the cheapest way of selling goods, particularly if the goods are worthless. SINCLAIR LEWIS

The consumer is not a moron. She is your wife. (Advice to advertising copywriters.) DAVID OGILVY

Lord Leverhulme once said that he knew very well that half the money spent by his company on advertising was wasted. The problem was to find out which half. *The Times*

ADVICE – *see also* OPINION.
You should never take advice from any man, however well he knows his subject, unless he also knows you. BALAAM

No man has ever yet discovered the way to give friendly advice to a woman, not even to his wife. HONORÉ DE BALZAC

To consult is to seek another's approval of a course already decided on. AMBROSE BIERCE

When a man comes to me for advice I find out the kind of advice he wants, and give it to him. JOSH BILLINGS

"As a grown man you should know better than to go round advising people." BERTOLT BRECHT

She generally gave herself very good advice (though she very seldom followed it). LEWIS CARROLL

In matters of religion and matrimony I never give any advice; because I will not have anybody's torments in this world or the next laid to my charge.
EARL OF CHESTERFIELD (1694–1773)

To ask advice is in nine cases out of ten to tout for flattery.
JOHN CHURTON COLLINS

This is the gist of what I know:
Give advice and buy a foe. PHYLLIS McGINLEY

I sometimes give myself admirable advice, but I am incapable of taking it. LADY MARY MONTAGU (1689–1762)

Since I have given you all this advice, I add this crowning precept, the most valuable of all. NEVER TAKE ANYBODY'S ADVICE. GEORGE BERNARD SHAW

Good advice is one of those injuries which a good man ought, if possible, to forgive. HORACE SMITH

No one wants advice – only corroboration.
JOHN STEINBECK

Only take this rule along,
Always to advise her wrong;
And reprove her when she's right;
She may then grow wise for spite.
JONATHAN SWIFT (1667–1745)

I have lived some thirty years on this planet, and I have yet to hear the first syllable of valuable or even earnest advice from my seniors. H. D. THOREAU

"I always pass on good advice. It is the only thing to do with it." OSCAR WILDE

AGE
Lately I appear
To have reached that stage
When people look old
Who are only my age. RICHARD ARMOUR

Mr Salteena was an elderly man of 42. DAISY ASHFORD

Old age is always fifteen years older than I am.
BERNARD M. BARUCH

I've never known a person to live to 110 or more, and then die, to be remarkable for anything else. JOSH BILLINGS

Old age is ... a lot of crossed-off names in your address book.
RONALD BLYTHE

It is advisable to choose your parents wisely. Most centenarians can boast of two parents who lived beyond seventy. MICHAEL BROOKE

The gardener's rule applies to youth and age:
When young "sow wild oats", but when old, grow sage.
H. J. BYRON

"You are old, Father William," the young man said,
"And your hair has become very white;
And yet you incessantly stand on your head –
Do you think at your age it is right?" LEWIS CARROLL

Growing old isn't so bad when you consider the alternative.
MAURICE CHEVALIER

The happiest time of life is between seventy and eighty, and I
advise everyone to hurry up and get there as soon as possible.
JOSEPH CHOATE (U.S. diplomat, died in 1917, aged 85.)

When a man falls into his anecdotage it is a sign for him to
retire. BENJAMIN DISRAELI

When you're older you're colder. A. G. ELLIOT

All would live long, but none would be old.
BENJAMIN FRANKLIN

To be seventy years young is sometimes far more cheerful and
hopeful than to be forty years old. O. W. HOLMES

A man over ninety is a great comfort to his elderly
neighbours... Young folks of sixty or seventy feel that the
enemy must get by him before getting near their camp.
O. W. HOLMES

You know you're getting old when the candles cost more than
the cake. BOB HOPE

Age is a question of mind over matter. If you don't mind, it
doesn't matter. DAN INGMAN

No man is ever old enough to know better.
HOLBROOK JACKSON

The inevitable result of any attempt to prolong youth is a
graceless old age. CLIVE JAMES

One of the two things that men who have lasted for one
hundred years always say: either that they have drunk whisky

and smoked all their lives, or that neither tobacco nor spirits ever made the slightest appeal to them. E. V. LUCAS

"I do not call myself really old yet. Not till a young woman offers me her seat in a railway compartment will that tragedy really be mine." E. V. LUCAS

Passing your 80th birthday is no great achievement. You just sit still and it happens. ANGUS McBEAN

Anyone can get old. All you have to do is to live long enough. GROUCHO MARX

Middle-age – by which I mean anything over twenty and under ninety. A. A. MILNE

Senescence begins
And middle age ends
The day your descendants
Outnumber your friends. OGDEN NASH

King David and King Solomon
   Led merry, merry lives,
With many, many concubines
   And many, many wives;
But when old age crept over them –
   With many, many qualms,
King Solomon wrote the Proverbs
   And King David wrote the Psalms. JAMES BALL NAYLOR

When you've reached a certain age and think that a face-lift or a trendy way of dressing will make you feel twenty years younger, remember – nothing can fool a flight of stairs. DENIS NORDEN

Walk sober off, before a sprightlier age

Comes tittering on, and shoves you from the stage.
ALEXANDER POPE (1688–1744)

It's no use growing older if you only learn new ways of misbehaving yourself. SAKI

Reminiscences make one feel so deliciously aged and sad. GEORGE BERNARD SHAW

One evil in old age is that you think every little illness is the beginning of the end. When a man expects to be arrested, every knock at the door is an alarm. SYDNEY SMITH

You are old, Father William, the young man cried,
    The few locks that are left you are grey.
You are hale, Father William, a hearty old man,
    Now tell me the reason, I pray. ROBERT SOUTHEY

The greatest problem of old age is the fear that it may go on too long. A. J. P. TAYLOR

It's silly to talk of old age; there's always a young person inside. SYBIL THORNDIKE

Life would be infinitely happier if we could only be born at the age of 80 and gradually approach 18. MARK TWAIN

When your friends being to flatter you on how young you look, it's a sure sign you're getting old. MARK TWAIN

If I'd known I was going to live to be 100 I would have taken better care of myself. ANON

ANCESTORS – *see also* RELATIONS.
"I can trace my ancestry back to a protoplasmal primordial atomic globule. My family pride is something inconceivable."
W. S. GILBERT

The family you come from isn't as important as the family you're going to have. RING W. LARDNER

To have an ancestor who was hanged for sheep-stealing perhaps gives me a certain social standing. ROBERT MORLEY

ANGER – *see also* ABUSE, CURSING, INSULTS.
Never forget what a man says to you when he's angry.
HENRY WARD BEECHER

A man in a passion rides a mad horse. BENJAMIN FRANKLIN

Peace of mind is better than giving them a piece of your mind.
J. P. McEVOY

Anger is not only inevitable; it is also necessary. Its absence means indifference, the most disastrous of human failings.
ARTHUR PONSONBY

If you strike a child, take care that you strike it in anger... A blow in cold blood neither can nor should be forgiven.
GEORGE BERNARD SHAW

ANIMALS – *see also* BIRDS, CATS AND DOGS, FISH, HORSE, HUNTING, INSECTS, RACING.
Elephant: a joker of the animal kingdom, having a flexible nose. AMBROSE BIERCE

Have you ever tried to get a quietish sort of dog to bark into a microphone? I had to pretend to be a dustman.
J. BASIL BOOTHROYD

[The deer in] Richmond Park... come up close to people without the least fuss, and they show a preference for vegetarians. KAREL CAPEK

I had a hippopotamus: I kept him in a shed
And fed him upon vitamins and vegetable bread . . .
He frolicked with the Rector in a dozen friendly tussles,
Who could not but remark upon his hippopotamuscles.
PATRICK BARRINGTON

He thought he saw a Banker's Clerk
  Descending from a bus:
He looked again, and found it was
  A Hippopotamus. LEWIS CARROLL

Orang-utans teach us that looks are not everything – but
darned near it. WILL CUPPY

Normal young tigers do not eat people. If eaten by a tiger you
may rest assured that he was abnormal. WILL CUPPY

The sloth lives his life upside down. He is perfectly
comfortable that way. If the blood rushes to his head, nothing
happens because there is nothing to work on. WILL CUPPY

The gnu's extraordinary movements... could only be
described as something like an acute attack of St Vitus's
Dance. GERALD DURRELL

Animals generally return the love you lavish on them by a swift bite in passing – not unlike friends and wives.
GERALD DURRELL

Beasts kill for hunger, men for pay. JOHN GAY (1685–1732)

Suburban foxes are not simply tame towards men. They are also damn supercilious. One pads amongst the azaleas in our garden at night, staring through the lounge windows to watch the *News at Ten*. RICHARD GORDON

It was Sunday morning (one a.m.), a not unusual time for some farmers, after a late Saturday night, to have a look round their stock and decide to send for the vet.
JAMES HERRIOT

Many birds and beasts are... as fit to go to Heaven as many human beings – people who talk of their seats there with as much confidence as if they had booked them at a box-office.
LEIGH HUNT

The camel has a single hump,
The dromedary two;
Or else the other way around,
I'm never sure. Are you? OGDEN NASH

A mouse that prayed for Allah's aid
Blasphemed when no such aid befell;
A Cat who feasted on that Mouse
Thought Allah managed vastly well. SAKI

"A relative of mine... spends his time producing improved breeds of sheep and pigs and chickens. So patronising and irritating to the Almighty, I should think." SAKI

"Anyone who works with animals in whatever capacity must be at least a bit dotty," says a zoo director friend.
DAVID TAYLOR (Zoo vet)

The man who has to muck out the monkeys is rarely if ever consulted when the architects roll up in their limousines to sketch out the new monkey-house. DAVID TAYLOR

The donkeys and the men, women, and children all eat and sleep in the same room, and are unclean, are ravaged with vermin, and are truly happy. MARK TWAIN

Man is the only animal that blushes – or needs to.
MARK TWAIN

Two beautiful deer came sauntering across the grounds and stopped and looked me over as if they thought of buying me.
MARK TWAIN

If, strolling forth, a beast you view
    Whose hide with spots is peppered,
As soon as it has leapt on you
    You'll know it is a leopard. CAROLYN WELLS

APOLOGY
Apologize: to lay the foundations for a future offence.
AMBROSE BIERCE

"I never apologize." (Major Saranoff)
GEORGE BERNARD SHAW

It's a good rule in life never to apologize. The right sort of people don't want apologies, and the wrong sort take a mean advantage of them. P. G. WODEHOUSE

ARCHITECTURE - see also ART, HOUSE AND HOME, LONDON.
Architecture approaches nearer than any other art to being irrevocable, because it is so difficult to get rid of.
G. K. CHESTERTON

All architecture is great architecture after sunset.
G. K. CHESTERTON

We shape our buildings; thereafter they shape us.
WINSTON S. CHURCHILL

If I had to say which was telling the truth about society, a speech by a Minister of Housing or the actual buildings put up in his time, I should believe the buildings.
KENNETH CLARK

A courageous and partly successful attempt to disguise a gasworks as a racquets court. PETER FLEMING (on the Shakespeare Memorial Theatre, Stratford-on-Avon.)

ARGUMENT - see also BIGOTRY, OPINION.
Mr Lloyd George [in a two-hour speech] was detected only once in the use of an argument. ARNOLD BENNETT

There is no arguing with Johnson, for when his pistol misses fire, he knocks you down with the butt end of it.
OLIVER GOLDSMITH

If you argue with an N.C.O., as all good Scotsmen must, you are insubordinate. IAN HAY

The only argument available with an east wind is to put on your overcoat. J. R. LOWELL

"Yes, but not in the South," with slight adjustments, will do for any argument about any place. STEPHEN POTTER

I dislike arguments of any kind. They are always vulgar, and often convincing. OSCAR WILDE

ARISTOCRACY – *see also* CLASS, EQUALITY, ETIQUETTE, MONEY.
Honour is a luxury for aristocrats, but it is a necessity for hall-porters. G. K. CHESTERTON

High rank involves no shame –
We boast an equal claim
With him of humble name
  To be respected. W. S. GILBERT

When everyone is somebody
Then no one's anybody. W. S. GILBERT

Titles distinguish the mediocre, embarrass the superior, and are disgraced by the inferior. GEORGE BERNARD SHAW

We adore titles and heredities in our hearts, and ridicule them with our mouths. That is our democratic privilege.
MARK TWAIN

ARMY – *see also* BEARDS, ENEMY, WAR.
If a soldier wishes to speak to an officer an introduction must be effected by a sergeant. IAN HAY

Three platoons out of four in our company are at present commanded by N.C.O's ... one of whom has been picked out of the ranks simply because he possesses a loud voice and a cake of soap. IAN HAY

There was a big route march on that morning and nearly the whole company had gone sick as a result. J. MACLAREN-ROSS

"Right-turn," I managed to get out. They all turned left.
J. MACLAREN-ROSS

ART – *see also* **ARCHITECTURE.**
Fig-leaf: An artist's trick by which the Nude's
Protected from the eyes of prudes. AMBROSE BIERCE

Any fool can paint a picture but it takes a wise man to be able to sell it. SAMUEL BUTLER

If you went round the National Portrait Gallery without knowing who the portraits were of, you would be as bored as if they were so much wall-paper. LORD DAVID CECIL

Auguste Renoir
Travelled afar
To find a model
He could codel. JONATHAN CLEMENTS

Here is a fact that never should be hid:
House painting came before the houses did.
Primitive man, who could not build at all,
Could paint good pictures on his cavern wall. A. P. HERBERT

He loved painting, all painting, indiscriminately. In a picture gallery he was like Turk in a harem; he adored them all.
ALDOUS HUXLEY

During the last eight years... he had worked his way industriously through cubism. Now he had come out on the other side. ALDOUS HUXLEY

"I must have gone on looking at pictures for ten years before I would honestly admit to myself that they merely bored me." ALDOUS HUXLEY

Art, like Nature, makes its own laws as it goes along. LAMBERT JEFFRIES

The business of art is to colour the mind; the business of science is to straighten it. LAMBERT JEFFRIES

"What are you painting?" I said. "Is it the Heavenly Child?" "No," he said, "it is a cow." STEPHEN LEACOCK

I have... several original Mona Lisas and all painted (according to the signature) by the great artist Kodak. SPIKE MILLIGAN

I took my children to see some of Henry Moore's chunky abstract sculptures in Hyde Park. My daughter Laura, 7, said, "Look, something's fallen off a Jumbo Jet." SPIKE MILLIGAN

Many painters and writers have made beautiful works out of repulsive subjects. Picasso enjoys making repulsive works out of beautiful subjects. RAYMOND MORTIMER

Art is a lie which makes us realize the truth. PABLO PICASSO

The women of the Italian masters are disgustingly fat, and their babies are on the verge of apoplexy.
R. C. ROBERTSON-GLASGOW

Troubetskoi worked convulsively, giving birth to the thing in agonies, hurling lumps of clay about ... He covered himself with plaster. He covered the carpets and curtains and pictures with plaster. He covered me with plaster.
GEORGE BERNARD SHAW

How often my soul visits the National Gallery, and how seldom I go there myself! LOGAN PEARSALL SMITH

BABIES – *see also* CHILDREN, PARENTS.
We have never understood the fear of some parents about babies getting mixed up in a hospital. What difference does it make as long as you get a good one? HEYWOOD BROUN

More twins are being born these days. Maybe it's because kids haven't the courage to come into the world alone.
STAN BURNS

Lullaby, O lullaby!
The brat will never shut an eye;
Hither come, some power divine!
Close his lids, or open mine! THOMAS HOOD

Give an average baby a fair chance, and if it doesn't do something it oughtn't to, a doctor should be called in at once.
J. K. JEROME

No baby is admired sufficiently to please the mother.
E. V. LUCAS

Only last year a gentleman – and, be it noted, a bachelor –
applied for a patent for a device for administering milk to
newborn babies. *Strand Magazine*

BALLET – *see also* DANCING.
I can think of nothing more kinky than a prince chasing a
swan around all night. ROBERT HELPMAN

If dancing is the expression of love-making it is the oddest in
the world, for the lady is (often) forgotten. The gentleman
capers by himself, and he expresses his passion by seeing how
many jumps he can take, how often he can quiver his feet
before he comes down, and how eminently he can stand on
one leg. LEIGH HUNT

BANKS – *see also* BUSINESS, MONEY.
If reapers sing while reaping, why should not auditors sing
while auditing and bankers while banking? If there are songs
for all the separate things that have to be done in a boat, why
are there not songs for all the separate things that have to be
done in a bank? G. K. CHESTERTON

George goes to sleep at a bank from ten to four each day,
except Saturdays, when they wake him up and put him
outside at two. J. K. JEROME

Most banks will gladly grant a loan,
    In fact they often speed it;
The only thing that they require
    Is proof that you don't need it. F. G. KERNAN

The manager got up and opened the door ... A big iron door
stood open at the side of the room.

"Good morning," I said, and stepped into the safe.
"Come out," said the manager coldly, and showed me the other way. STEPHEN LEACOCK

At the bank counter queue the villain of the piece is easily identified: he is the man with the large canvas bag containing £486.35 in five and ten pence pieces which he is about to pay in, along with eighteen assorted cheques which he wishes to be credited to a variety of accounts. OLIVER PRITCHETT

Banks don't make pleasant shareholders.
JULIAN SHUCKBURGH (publisher)

BEARDS – *see also* **BODY, FACE, HAIR.**
He had a chin on which large numbers of hairs weakly curled and clustered to cover its retreat. MAX BEERBOHM

Charlemagne was renowned for the length of his beard. It was said that he could kneel on it, though it is not recorded why this was necessary. NICHOLAS BENTLEY

Beard: The hair that is commonly cut off by those who justly execrate the absurd Chinese custom of shaving the head.
AMBROSE BIERCE

Among the Romans all foreigners were called barbarians because most of the tribes with which the Romans had acquaintance were bearded. AMBROSE BIERCE

"As I entered the ballroom," writes a young Victorian lady, "I saw along the wall a row of curly brown beards – a truly beautiful sight." ARTHUR BRYANT

The best after-shave is cold water, but clever industrial chemists have persuaded many men to put all kinds of muck on their faces. LAMBERT JEFFRIES

Alexander the Great thought that the beards of the soldiery
afforded convenient handles for the enemy to lay hold of...
and he ordered the whole of his army to be closely shaven.
CHARLES MACKAY

Beware of long arguments and long beards.
GEORGE SANTAYANA

An irregular greying beard was a decoration to a face that
badly needed assistance. EDGAR WALLACE

BEAUTY – *see also* **BODY, FACE, WOMAN.**
When all the vanishing cream has vanished,
    And the last lone lipstick's died,
Will beauty then be banished –
    Or be intensified? A. W. BIRD

All heiresses are beautiful. JOHN DRYDEN (1631–1700)

Beauty, when most uncloth'd, is clothèd best.
PHINEAS FLETCHER (1582–1650)

In beauty faults conspicuous grow;
The smallest speck is seen on snow. JOHN GAY (1685–1732)

A queen devoid of beauty is not queen. VICTOR HUGO

I'm tired of all this nonsense about beauty being only skin deep... What do you want – an adorable pancreas? JEAN KERR

"I always say, beauty is only sin deep." SAKI

The saying that beauty is but skin deep is but a skin-deep saying. HERBERT SPENCER

BED – *see also* DREAMS, IDLENESS, SLEEP.
My solution for the problem of habitual accidents... is for everyone to stay in bed all day. Even then there is always the chance that you will fall out. ROBERT BENCHLEY

I could keep out of bed all right if I once got out. It is the wrenching away of the head from the pillow that I find so hard. J. K. JEROME

My bedfellows are cough and cramp; we sleep three in a bed. CHARLES LAMB

There is not a single proverb in favour of early rising that appeals to the higher nature of man. ROBERT LYND

No human being believes that any other human being has a right to be in bed when he himself is up. ROBERT LYND

The information has only recently come my way that the late Mr Gladstone, preparing himself for slumber in No. 10, had his hot water bottle filled, not with hot water in the ordinary way... but with, as a variation, hot soup. ARTHUR MARSHALL

Do *not* allow the bride to select the side upon which she

wishes to spend the night ... It is a tacit admission that she is
the boss in bed, an unthinkable proposition.
JOHN MARSHALL

"The sun streamed into my room, and I said, It's a sin not to
get up on a morning like this. And the more I said I ought
to get up, the more delightful I found it to lie in bed."
W. SOMERSET MAUGHAM

BEGGING
Show your most revolting scar;
    People never weary of it.
The more nauseous you are
    More their pity – and your profit. J. ELROY FLECKER

BIGOTRY – *see also* ARGUMENT, OPINION.
A bigot is one who is obstinately and zealously attached to an
opinion that you do not entertain. AMBROSE BIERCE

A man convinced against his will
Is of the same opinion still. SAMUEL BUTLER (1612–80)

The more you are in the right, the more natural that everyone
else should be bullied into thinking likewise.
GEORGE ORWELL

BIRDS – *see also* ANIMALS, CATS AND DOGS, FISH, HORSE, INSECTS.
All I know of birds to this date is that sparrows are the ones
that are not pigeons. ALAN COREN

The Love Bird is one hundred percent faithful to his mate –
who is locked into the same cage. WILL CUPPY

The loon bobs up in the surf on dark nights, ruins your

summer with a burst of wild maniacal laughter... and
wonders why people shoot at him. WILL CUPPY

The wren-box problem is becoming more acute each year, for
wrens now demand better housing conditions and labour-
saving devices. WILL CUPPY

The cuckoo is no credit to his race: his arrogance and want of
responsibility are deplorable; and he sings the same song so
many times over that one is ashamed of him. E. V. LUCAS

There is nothing in which the birds differ more from man
than the way in which they can build and yet leave a
landscape as it was before. ROBERT LYND

Why does a silly bird go on saying "chiff-chaff" all day long?
Is it happiness or hiccups? A. A. MILNE

"A fly can't bird, but a bird can fly." A. A. MILNE

Cogg would suddenly stand stock still. "Listen," he would
say. Some feeble quack would be heard from the willow
beyond the pond. "That's an easy one to tell. The frog-

pippit." Then he would add, as a safety measure, "as I believe they call it in these parts." STEPHEN POTTER

If you hear the nightingale before the cuckoo, your love affair will prosper. JACK THOMAS

We were surprised how closely the cuckoo imitated the clock – and yet, of course, it could never have heard a clock. MARK TWAIN

I had started by imitating a parrot, which is unusual, in that a parrot is supposed to imitate you. By taking the initiative you allow the parrot no alternative but to be itself, which proves again that attack is often the best defence. PETER USTINOV

BOATS – *see also* ACCIDENTS, HOLIDAYS, SEASICKNESS, SEASIDE, TRAVEL.
Margo took over the steering... In a crisis she would get flurried and forget that to turn right one had to put the tiller over to the left. GERALD DURRELL

It was impossible to use the communal bath [on board ship] as it was never really clean and always looked as though a large grizzly bear had recently bathed in it and lost half his fur in doing so. JACQUIE DURRELL

"There is nothing – absolutely nothing – half so much worth doing as simply messing about in boats."
KENNETH GRAHAME

I was thinking of other things, and forgot, as anyone might easily understand, that I was steering, and the consequence was that we got mixed up a good deal with the towpath.
J. K. JEROME

A ship is worse than a jail. There is, in a jail, better air, better

company, better conveniency of every kind: and a ship has the additional disadvantage of being in danger.
SAMUEL JOHNSON

Ship's cooks have two peculiarities – a most extraordinary flow of language and an endless capacity for song.
F. D. OMMANNEY

We began sinking, and there is no sight more ludicrous than eight men, with a small ninth the size of a jockey, settling gracefully into the water in Indian file. PETER USTINOV

BODY – *see also* BEARDS, BEAUTY, CLOTHES, FACE, HAIR, OBESITY.
I am always meeting idealists with very long necks.
G. K. CHESTERTON

My hand from finger-tip to wrist measures exactly seven inches. Another five inches and it would become a foot.
BERT DOUGLAS

What a comfort it would be if one could bring air cushions into school chapel. ALDOUS HUXLEY

She was built in the way they used to build cars at that time – all the weight at the back. DENIS NORDEN

Everything below her neck was so unconfined that when her feet came to a halt, the rest of her took perceptibly longer to settle down. DENIS NORDEN

His flabby, redundant figure sat up in bewildered semi-consciousness, like an ice-cream that has been taught to beg.
SAKI

BOOKS – *see also* CRITICISM, LIBRARIES, POETRY, PROSE, QUOTATIONS, WRITING.
When I am dead, I hope it may be said:

"His sins were scarlet, but his books were read."
HILAIRE BELLOC

If one took a volume of Chaucer or Shelley from that row of books, its absence irritated the mind like a gap in a man's front teeth. G. K. CHESTERTON

A novel, according to my taste, does not come into the moderately good class unless it contains some person whom one can thoroughly love – and if a pretty woman, all the better. CHARLES DARWIN

He knew everything about literature except how to enjoy it.
JOSEPH HELLER

"Books," he said – "books. One reads so many... I must have read twenty or thirty tons of them in the last five years."
ALDOUS HUXLEY

If you believe everything you read, better not read.
GEORGE JOHNSTONE

Many modern novels have a beginning, a muddle, and an end. PHILIP LARKIN

There is a legend that they [the books of the great Alexandrian Library] were deliberately burned by order of the Caliph – because if they contradicted the Koran they were heretical, while if they agreed they were superfluous.
PATRICK MOORE

His book hit the world with all the impact of a feather falling on to a piece of damp blotting-paper. PATRICK MOORE

By not hitting my sister for three months, and weeding the garden... by these and other deeds I saved enough money to buy the book *(The Coral Island)*. E. ARNOT ROBERTSON

BOREDOM

A bore is a person who talks when you wish him to listen.
AMBROSE BIERCE

I love the man who knows it all,
From East to West, from North to South,
Who knows all things both great and small,
And tells them with his tiresome mouth. R. J. BURDETTE

Society is now one polished horde,
Formed of two mighty tribes – the *Bores* and *Bored*.
LORD BYRON

"Can there be anything more boring than this sweet country boredom?" ANTON CHEKHOV

Everyone is a bore to someone. LAMBERT JEFFRIES

Coming away from dinner at a house noted for its dullness, Dumas père was asked by someone if he had not been dreadfully bored. "I should have been," he replied, "if *I* hadn't been there." E. V. LUCAS

The capacity of human beings to bore one another seems to be vastly greater than that of any other animals.
H. L. MENCKEN

"Christ," said Gunner White, "I *must* be bored. I just thought of Catford." SPIKE MILLIGAN

He had a habit of choosing a subject and then droning round and round it like an inaccurate bomb-aimer.
NANCY MITFORD

If you decline the verb "to be a bore", it goes: "You are a bore" – "he is a bore" – "they are bores". You very rarely hear "I am a bore". FRANK MUIR

His talents lay so thoroughly in the direction of being uninteresting that even as an eye-witness of the massacre of St Bartholomew he would probably have infused a flavour of boredom into his description of the event. SAKI

BUSINESS – *see also* BANKS.
In matters of commerce the fault of the Dutch
Is giving too little and asking too much. GEORGE CANNING

"Business? That's simply other people's money."
ALEXANDRE DUMAS

"Our modern business men are as grossly overtaxed physically as fiscally (said Sir Lancelot)... They simply eat and drink too much, smoke like the borough incinerator, and get no exercise beyond winding up their alarm clocks."
RICHARD GORDON

My two new assistants are incompetent dullards, so they should do very well in British industry. MICHAEL GREEN

The trouble with mixin' business with pleasure is that pleasure allus comes to the top. KIN HUBBARD

In my business hours I avoid fatigue. I do this by not doing too much work – the only trustworthy recipe. E. V. KNOX

"I'm going to start at the bottom and work my way down."
P. G. WODEHOUSE

CARDS – *see also* GAMBLING.
Never play cards with any man named "Doc".
NELSON ALGREN

A Major-General across the hall was desperately trying to

create three no-trumps where God had only created two.
A. G. MACDONELL

"I hate people who play Bridge as though they were at a funeral, and knew their feet were getting wet."
W. SOMERSET MAUGHAM

"It's maddening when you're playing Patience and people won't leave you alone." W. SOMERSET MAUGHAM

Where each player receives a hand of thirteen cards, the total possible number of different hands which may thus be dealt is greater than six hundred millions. G. A. ROSSETTI

(No one) who has wrestled with a self-adjusting card-table can ever be quite the man he once was. JAMES THURBER

CARS – *see also* **MOTORING, RAILWAY, ROADS, TRAVEL.**
Put a man behind the wheel of a car, they say, and his personality really starts to show itself. ALAN AYCKBOURN

The mechanic said that if she'd been a horse he'd have had to shoot her, but as things were, he could probably fix her up so that she wouldn't actually fall to pieces in the street.
J. BASIL BOOTHROYD

The most spectacular experience I had at this time was having to use a car for twenty-four hours that could only go down hill in reverse. MARY BRANCKER

The car provided was a small Fiat... The more important drawback to this car was that it was totally invisible to adjacent bus drivers. MARY BRANCKER

The London cab driver is forbidden by law to have an interior mirror, so that he can't see what's going on on the back seat.
LEN DEIGHTON

A conservation area is a place where you can't build a garage but you can build a motorway. JAMES GLADSTONE

Every car owner is a liar. He exaggerates his speed, the number of miles he goes to the gallon of petrol, and his prowess as a hill-climber. ALDOUS HUXLEY

The starter went wrong, and after a week or two I also lost the starting-handle. So the only possible way to start the car was to put her in gear, give her a push, and when the motor started, jump in and drive away. At the beginning it happened occasionally that the car ran faster than I did. GEORGE MIKES

The only part of the car that didn't make a noise when in motion was the hooter. DENIS NORDEN

After I'd switched off the ignition the whole inside of the bonnet would go on shaking for about three minutes, like a dog coming out of the water. DENIS NORDEN

CATS AND DOGS – *see also* **ANIMALS, BIRDS, FISH, HORSE, INSECTS.**
The dog's all right in the car usually, but lately he's been

getting bored and he's learnt to push the horn button with his nose. ALAN AYCKBOURN

The only fault I have to find with a dog is that he doesn't live to be a hundred. LEWIS CAREY

I like very quiet doggies who never bark, never bite, and hardly ever move. NAT GUBBINS

Cat lovers can be readily identified ... No matter what they wear, their clothes always look old and well used.
ERIC GURNEY

"He leads a dog's life," people cry –
  But why?...
All day you do exactly as you feel;
You sleep before, and after, every meal.
  Things would be said
  If I had so much bed! A. P. HERBERT

Montmorency's ambition in life is to get in the way and be sworn at. If he can squirm in anywhere where he particularly is not wanted ... he feels his day has not been wasted.
J. K. JEROME

I knew a couple of elderly spinsters who had a sort of German sausage on legs which they called a dog. They used to wash its face with warm water every morning. J. K. JEROME

Really fat dogs and cats more often than not are owned by people who are on the tubby side themselves. There just has to be a moral there somewhere. MICHAEL STOCKMAN

If you try (on a bicycle) to run over a dog, he knows how to avoid you; but if you try to miss him, he doesn't know how to calculate. MARK TWAIN

I tried to convince Calvin (the cat), while he was eating the

bird, that he was doing wrong; for he is a reasonable cat and understands everything but the binomial theory.
C. DUDLEY WARNER

An Airedale, erect beside the chauffeur of a Rolls-Royce,
Often gives you the impression he's there from choice.
E. B. WHITE

Percy was the dog's name... His guiding rule in life was "If it moves, bite it". P. G. WODEHOUSE

CHARM
They charmed it with smiles and soap. LEWIS CARROLL

How happy could I be with either
Were t'other dear charmer away! JOHN GAY (1685–1732)

Oozing charm from every pore
He oiled his way across the floor. ALAN JAY LERNER

CHASTITY – *see also* ADULTERY, SEX.
She is chaste who was never asked the question.
WILLIAM CONGREVE (1670–1729)

"It doesn't suit women to be promiscuous."
"It doesn't suit men for women to be promiscuous."
NOEL COWARD

The very ice of chastity is in them.
WILLIAM SHAKESPEARE *(As You Like It)*

CHILDREN – *see also* **BABIES, EDUCATION, PARENTS, SCHOOLS.**
"Those damned sweets! Why can't they put them in their ugly little mouths? Instead of all over my floor!"
ALAN AYCKBOURN

Far from cementing a marriage, children more frequently disrupt it. Child rearing is on the whole an expensive and unrewarding bore. NIGEL BALCHIN

A boy does not put his hand into his pocket until every other means of gaining his end has failed. J. M. BARRIE

Godolphin Horne was Nobly Born;
He held the Human Race in Scorn...
Alas! That such affected tricks
Should flourish in a Child of Six. HILAIRE BELLOC

There are two classes of travel – first class and with children.
ROBERT BENCHLEY

Children on a night boat seem to be built of hardier stock...
They stay awake later, get up earlier, and are heavier on their feet. ROBERT BENCHLEY

People who say they sleep like a baby usually don't have one.
LEO. J. BURKE

How many children have acquired a bad habit as a result of having it attributed to them! MICHAEL BURN

Impress your children with a deep sense of their inferiority. You carry so many more guns than they do that they cannot fight you. This is called moral influence. SAMUEL BUTLER

The only way to stop the children from nagging to be taken to Disneyworld was either to go, or to strangle them (a close decision). ALAN COREN

It must have been surprising, and, I should have thought, nauseating, to see a little boy of nine in a white sailor suit flitting about a small wooden stage, employing, with instinctive accuracy, the gestures and tricks of a professional soubrette. NOEL COWARD (on himself)

As soon as children are good the mothers are scared, and think they are going to die. R. W. EMERSON

Anybody who hates children and dogs can't be all bad.
W. C. FIELDS

Teach your child to hold his tongue; he'll learn fast enough to speak. BENJAMIN FRANKLIN

Father heard the children scream,
So he threw them in the stream,
Saying as he drowned the third,
"Children should be seen, *not* heard!" HARRY GRAHAM

Children are a great comfort in your old age – and they help you to reach it faster. LIONEL KAUFFMAN

I love children. Especially when they cry, for then someone takes them away. NANCY MITFORD

Both the aunt and the children were conversational in a limited, persistent way. Most of the aunt's remarks seemed to begin with "Don't", and nearly all of the children's remarks began with "Why?" SAKI

Hushabye Babies
(Hush quite a lot)
Bad Babies get Rabies
(And have to be shot).
W. C. SELLAR & R. J. YEATMAN

Physically there is nothing to distinguish human society from the farmyard except that children are more troublesome and costly than chickens. GEORGE BERNARD SHAW

I must have been an insufferable child; all children are.
GEORGE BERNARD SHAW

What is more enchanting than the voices of young people when you can't hear what they say? LOGAN PEARSALL SMITH

I like very much people telling me about their childhood, but they'll have to be quick or else I'll be telling them about mine.
DYLAN THOMAS

I can never remember whether it snowed for six days and six nights when I was twelve or whether it snowed for twelve days and twelve nights when I was six. DYLAN THOMAS

The irritating thing about badly behaved children is that they so often make as orderly and valuable men and women as the other kind. MARK TWAIN

Why should I want a Society for the Prevention of Cruelty to Children to prosper, when there is a baby downstairs that kept me awake several hours last night with no pretext but a desire to make trouble. MARK TWAIN

The main purpose of children's parties is to remind you that there are children more awful than your own.
KATHERINE WHITEHORN

Before I married I had six theories about bringing up

children, but no children; now I have six children and no theories. ANON

CHRISTMAS – *see also* CHURCH, RELIGION.
This is a play about... jealousy and self-deception. And greed and envy and lust and gluttony. Just an average family Christmas. ALAN AYCKBOURN

Christmas: a day set apart and consecrated to gluttony, drunkenness, maudlin sentiment, gift-taking, and public dullness. AMBROSE BIERCE

When I'm King there will be a law that no shop will be allowed to sell anything Christmassy until December 1st.
PAUL DANIELS

I have a carefully-worked-out plan for doing the Christmas shopping. It's called panic. PAUL DANIELS

Christmas has come, let's eat and drink –
This is no time to sit and think. W. H. DAVIES

"Every idiot who goes about with Merry Christmas on his lips should be boiled with his own pudding, and buried with a stake of holly through his heart." CHARLES DICKENS

I am more and more convinced that Scrooge was one of the most sensible men that I have ever read about.
MICHAEL GREEN

If I sent a Christmas card to Gilbert Harding he would add to the words "from Hubert Gregg" the words "and Gilbert Harding", and send it to someone else. HUBERT GREGG

"Novelty" is the one quality required for Christmas games...
If a game is novel it is enough. To the manager of a toy

department the continued vogue of cricket must be very bewildering. A. A. MILNE

If you send Christmas cards too early it looks as if you are simply soliciting cards in return. If you send them too late it looks more like a Panic Response than a Message of Goodwill. OLIVER PRITCHETT

CHURCH – *see also* CHRISTMAS, FUNERALS, HEAVEN, RELIGION.
"Just been to church... Pay my respects, you know. I like to go once a year, that's all. Just in case. Keep the options open, eh?" ALAN AYCKBOURN

To Mr Rawlinson's church... and very great store of fine women there is in this church, more than I know anywhere else. SAMUEL PEPYS (1633–1703)

There was an old fellow of Fratton
Who would go to church with his hat on.
  "If I wake up," he said,
  With my hat on my head,
I shall know that it hasn't been sat on." ANON

CINEMA – *see also* TELEVISION AND RADIO, THEATRE.
A sixpenny seat meant that you occupied a hard bench almost within touching distance of the brass rail enclosing the orchestra pit, and here the screen was enormous. Gloria Swanson's eyes looked like Siberian lakes.
R. F. DELDERFIELD

I want a movie that starts with an earthquake and works up to a climax. SAM GOLDWYN (attributed)

The length of a film should be directly related to the endurance of the human bladder. ALFRED HITCHCOCK

CLASS – *see also* **ARISTOCRACY, ARMY, EQUALITY, MONEY.**
He claimed that the working-class man was the salt of the earth. He spoke with personal knowledge; he was a working-class man himself. LAMBERT JEFFRIES

I know people who secretly visit evening elocution classes in order to pick up a cockney accent. GEORGE MIKES

No one can make you feel inferior unless you consent. ELEANOR ROOSEVELT

Marx sought to replace natural antagonisms by class antagonisms. H. G. WELLS

When working-class people throw bottles and crockery at each other they quite often score hits; middle- or upper-class people seldom, if ever. MICHAEL WHARTON

CLOTHES – *see also* **BODY, FASHION, JEWELLERY.**
A little boy and a little girl were looking at a picture of Adam and Eve. "Which is which?" one asked. "I don't know," said the other, "but I could tell if they had their clothes on." SAMUEL BUTLER

Spent six consecutive weeks, without stopping,
In one continuous round of shopping...
Yet when we last met there was utter despair
Because she had nothing whatever to wear!
WILLIAM ALLEN BUTLER

Amid much cheering Mother removed her housecoat and stood revealed in all her glory, clad in the bathing-costume which made her look, as Larry pointed out, like a sort of marine Albert Memorial. GERALD DURRELL

For fifty years pyjamas were manufactured almost exclusively in broad coloured stripes which reduced men's sexual attractiveness in the bedroom to that of multi-coloured zebras. MARY EDEN

When a woman wears a low-cut gown, what does she expect you to do: look or not look? WILLIAM FEATHER

Nothing makes a man look so supremely ridiculous as losing his hat. J. K. JEROME

Apart from a few African ladies, from whom it would be but a glimpse of the obvious, "I have nothing to wear" really means "I have plenty of things to wear but I don't know how to wear them." JOHN MARSHALL

The kilt is an unrivalled garment for fornication and diarrhoea. JOHN MASTERS

"It suits you very well, dear."
"It's had long enough to get used to me!" A. A. MILNE

Below his kilt a self-respecting Highlander wore – and still wears – shoes and socks. FRANK MUIR

A dress has no purpose unless it makes a man want to take it off. FRANÇOISE SAGAN

Do not let penguins embarrass you if they happen to drop in when you are just sitting down to dinner. Evening dress is quite optional in Arctic Circles. W. C. SELLAR & R. J. YEATMAN

Some people are born with a sense of how to clothe themselves, others acquire it, others look as if their clothes had been thrust upon them. SAKI

"All dress is fancy dress, isn't it, except our natural skins."
GEORGE BERNARD SHAW

As martyrs burn for Christ, so ladies freeze for fashion.
C. H. SPURGEON

What struck me most when I first visited the House of Lords was the extraordinarily careless manner in which the peers were attired. They appeared to be a procession of savants and market-gardeners. H. BEERBOHM TREE

COLLECTING
When a thing is old, broken, and useless we throw it on the dust-heap, but when it is sufficiently old, sufficiently broken, and sufficiently useless we give money for it. SAMUEL BUTLER

If you had the true collector's temperament you would know that ... to give anything away without regretting it is quite an impossibility. E. V. LUCAS

CONJURING
Listen to your friends' criticisms of your performance. If they make sense, throw out any doubtful tricks. If they don't make sense, keep the doubtful tricks and throw out your friends.
LOU DERMAN

Are you indeed that Lady Psyche who
At children's parties drove the conjurer wild,
Explaining all his tricks before he did them? W. S. GILBERT

There is one very annoying circumstance, when at the

conclusion of a trick the person who has selected a card says, "Oh dear, I've forgotten what it was!" LOUIS HOFFMANN

You have to be honest to make a living deceiving people. ANON

COOKING – *see also* EATING.
It is impossible to combine the heating of milk with any other pursuit whatever. H. F. ELLIS

The speed at which boiling milk rises from the bottom of the pan to any point beyond the top is greater than the speed at which the human brain and hand can combine to snatch the confounded thing off. H. F. ELLIS

An unwatched pot boils immediately. H. F. ELLIS

Heaven sends us good meat, but the Devil sends cooks. DAVID GARRICK

She was a good cook, as cooks go; and as cooks go, she went. SAKI

COUNTRYSIDE – *see also* LONDON, WALKING.
The countryside is laid out in a haphazard, sloppy fashion, offensive to the tidy mind. ALAN BRIEN

I purchased one of the few tracts of genuine swamp in the New Forest, together with a small cottage sinking picturesquely into it. ALAN COREN

A pleasant excursion to collect wild flowers . . . We collected a daisy and fifty-nine things that weren't. ALAN COREN

"Farming seems to be mostly indecency and cruelty," said Anne. ALDOUS HUXLEY

"I might have ploughed that one myself," said his father admiringly on one occasion. "If I'd been blindfolded and short of one arm and with a team of horses that rocketed about like steeplechasers." A. G. MACDONELL

Dr Johnson detested Brighton Downs, "because it was a country so truly desolate that if one had a mind to hang oneself for desperation at having to live there, it would be difficult to find a tree on which to fasten the rope."
HESTER PIOZZI

CRICKET – *see also* **GAMES, RACING, SPORT, TENNIS.**
"I just wanted to find out who we were playing."
WARWICK ARMSTRONG (Australian 1921 Test captain, seen looking at a newspaper while fielding in the deep.)

Dr W. G. Grace
Had hair all over his face.
Lord! How the people cheered
When a ball got lost in his beard! E. C. BENTLEY

In my third summer term at school I developed a capacity, owing to my great height and increasing weight, for bowling so fast that our own wicket-keeper frequently buried his head in his gloves to get out of the way. PATRICK CAMPBELL

Of all games and sports, cricket appears to be most trying to the temper, for a player cannot lose his wicket without being put out. THOMAS HOOD

I ran for a catch
With the sun in my eyes, sir . . .
Now I wear a black patch
And a nose such a size, sir! COULSON KERNAHAN

Shakespeare was evidently a keen follower of the national game... The most conclusive evidence is to be found in his most frequent stage direction, *Exeunt omnes* (all out). Unfortunately the Bard had no head for figures, so we never learn the score. D. L. LOVELL-CLARKE

Mr Pollock (American baseball enthusiast), striking the first ball he received towards square leg, threw down his bat, and himself set off at a great rate in the direction of cover-point.
A. G. MACDONELL

The first ball he received he lashed at wildly and hit it straight up in the air to an enormous height... Up and up it went and then at the top it seemed to hang motionless in the air, poised like a hawk, fighting, as it were, a heroic but forlorn battle against the chief invention of Sir Isaac Newton.
A. G. MACDONELL

My own speciality... was to use the bat the wrong way round and present the triangular side to the ball. The results pass all expectation, the ball flying off quite unpredictably.
ARTHUR MARSHALL

Cricket is the only game where the major part of the team can just idle around and watch a few of their number do the work.
GEORGE MIKES

My father was one of the few umpires of my experience who appealed along with the bowler. MICHAEL PARKINSON

He often fielded at deep third man on the slope... He could not see the game, and the other players could not see him. He got his own back for this indignity by rolling the ball in a fresh cow pat. JAMES PRESTON

If the French *noblesse* had been capable of playing cricket with their peasants their chateaux would never have been burnt. G. M. TREVELYAN

Here is a game so doggedly peculiar and dangerous that no foreign nations... have ever adopted it. PETER USTINOV

To the spectators, cricket is more a therapy than a sport. It is like watching fish dart about a pool. MICHAEL WALE

CRIME – *see also* MURDER, PRISON, STEALING.
He is capable of any crime, from reviling the classics to diverting water-courses. ERNEST BRAMAH

My object all sublime
I shall achieve in time –
To make the punishment fit the crime. W. S. GILBERT

In the Army, "crime" may range from being unshaven on parade... to irrevocably perforating your rival in love with a bayonet. IAN HAY

"Crime doesn't pay; so stop being a criminal and we'll pay you." EUGENE IONESCO

Much as he is opposed to law-breaking he is not bigoted about it. DAMON RUNYON

CRITICISM – *see also* **ABUSE, BOOKS, INSULTS, THEATRE, WRITING.**
One cannot attack a bad book without showing off.
W. H. AUDEN

Friendly attacks should begin with faint praise, but be careful not to use adjectives or phrases of which the publisher can make use in advertisements. JOHN BETJEMAN

At any London first night you'll see the critics creeping off to the pub half-way through Act III. Of course, they pretend they've got to catch the early editions. J. BASIL BOOTHROYD

Hope constancy in wind, or corn in chaff,
Believe a woman or an epitaph,
Or any other thing that's false, before
You trust in critics. LORD BYRON

Alexander Woolcott, in a rage, has all the tenderness and restraint of a newly caged cobra. NOEL COWARD

Reading John Updike's *Couples* is like studying science while watching pornographic movies put together from random scraps on the cutting-room floor. JOHN GARDNER

The critic is often an unsuccessful author, almost always an inferior one. LEIGH HUNT

There is a type of critic whose attitude suggests that the book he is reviewing was written by his kind permission, and that the author has grossly abused the privilege.
LAMBERT JEFFRIES

You may scold a carpenter who has made you a bad table, though you cannot make a table. SAMUEL JOHNSON

"The next item on the programme," says the newspaper

report unkindly, "was quite a pleasing one. It was the interval." LOUIS NIKOLA

This is not a novel to be tossed aside lightly. It should be thrown with great force. DOROTHY PARKER

In Newstatesmanship, the critic is invariably a tremendous specialist in the subject under review, and must at all costs be more so. than the author of the book discussed.
STEPHEN POTTER

The worst convention of the criticism of the theatre current at that time (c. 1900)... was that a playwright is a person whose business is to make unwholesome confectionary out of cheap emotion. GEORGE BERNARD SHAW

Most writers... accept vituperation...as a healthy counterpoint to unintelligent praise. EVELYN WAUGH

CURSING – *see also* **ABUSE, ANGER, INSULTS.**
He cursed him in eating, he cursed him in drinking,
He cursed him in coughing, in sneezing, in winking;
He cursed him in sitting, in standing, in lying;
He cursed him in walking, in riding, in flying,
He cursed him in living, he cursed him in dying!
R. H. BARHAM

Swear not at all, for, for thy curse
Thine enemy is none the worse. A. H. CLOUGH

"The sale of our penny curses, especially on Saturday nights, is tremendous. We can't turn them out fast enough."
W. S. GILBERT

The Eskimos have no words for cursing, and Nansen says also no words of opprobrium, such as liar, scoundrel, or rowdy. WILFRED GRENFELL

We went slap into that punt, where those three old men were sitting... They cursed us – not with a common cursory curse, but with long carefully-thought-out, comprehensive curses, that embraced the whole of our careers, and went away into the distant future. J. K. JEROME

He turned and cursed the Jackaroo, he cursed him alive
    or dead,
From the soles of his great unwieldy feet to the crown of
    his ugly head. A. B. PATERSON
    (Jackaroo – new man on Australian sheep station.)

I know how to curse: the red plague rid you
For learning me your language!
WILLIAM SHAKESPEARE *(The Tempest)*

The devil damn thee black, thou cream-faced loon!
WILLIAM SHAKESPEARE *(Macbeth)*

A witch of full powers is urgently sought to lift a 73-year-old curse and help restore the fortunes of an afflicted nobleman. Employment genuinely offered.
The Times, March 1967 (advertisement)

CYNICISM – *see also* PESSIMISM.
A cynic is a blackguard whose faulty vision sees things as they are, not as they ought to be. AMBROSE BIERCE

Cynicism is an unpleasant way of saying the truth.
LILLIAN HELLMAN

Cynicism is the armour of the idealist. LAMBERT JEFFRIES

A cynic is a sentimentalist afraid of himself.
LAMBERT JEFFRIES

The worst government is the most moral. One composed of cynics is often very tolerant and humane. H. L. MENCKEN

"I like him," I replied. "He restores my cynicism about the human race." CHARLES MERCER

The power of accurate observation is often called cynicism by those who have not got it. GEORGE BERNARD SHAW

Cynicism is humour in ill-health. H. G. WELLS

"A cynic is a man who knows the price of everything and the value of nothing." OSCAR WILDE

DANCING – *see also* BALLET.
I've no desire to prove anything by dancing. I just dance.
FRED ASTAIRE

Dance: to leap about to the sound of tittering music, preferably with your neighbour's wife or daughter.
AMBROSE BIERCE

My conversation on the dance floor is pretty realistic and stereotyped. It consists in me saying, "I'm terribly sorry, was

that your foot?" and her limping off to the first-aid tent.
J. BASIL BOOTHROYD

"Dancing?... 'Tis certainly a Barbarian exercise, and of savage origin." FANNY BURNEY

Many will not allow men and women to dance together, because it is a provocation to lust.
ROBERT BURTON (1577–1640)

"I've danced with a man, who's danced with a girl, who's danced with the Prince of Wales." HERBERT FARJEON

She clapped me to her bosom like a belladonna plaster and pushed me on to the dance floor... It was like being lashed to an upholstered pneumatic drill. RICHARD GORDON

The choreographer convinced me that I looked like Fred Astaire, and I never doubted it. But when I saw the film... I thought I looked like a little hippopotamus shaking its hooves. BILL HOSKINS

Fifty years from now the only one of today's dancers who will be remembered is Fred Astaire. GENE KELLY

Dancing with her was like moving a piano. RING W. LARDNER

Dancing is wonderful training for girls; it's the first way you learn to guess what a man is going to do before he does it. CHRISTOPHER MORLEY

Most dancing partnerships lead to marriage. What could be more moral than that? FRANK AND PEGGY SPENCER

Everyone knows that the real business of a ball is either to look out for a wife, to look after a wife, or to look after somebody else's wife. R. S. SURTEES

I found the courage to decline a charming invitation to dance with the Queen (or should it be a command?), by warning her of the physical dangers attendant on such an initiative... Under Elizabeth I it would no doubt have cost me my head.
PETER USTINOV

Dancing is the perpendicular expression of a horizontal desire. ANON

Dancing the Twist is just as if you'd dropped a cigarette end on the floor and were grinding it out with the toe of your shoe.
ANON

Many people nowadays don't dance; they just wriggle about.
ANON

DEATH – *see also* **EPITAPHS, FUNERALS, MURDER.**
It's not that I'm afraid to die. I just don't want to be there when it happens. WOODY ALLEN

There have been times when I've thought about suicide – but with my luck it would probably turn out to be only a temporary solution. WOODY ALLEN

What I like about Clive
Is that he is no longer alive.
There is a great deal to be said
For being dead. E. C. BENTLEY

She said, "This looks a healthy village – do people often die here." "No, only once." BILLY BURDEN

The strangest whim has seized me... After all
    I think I will not hang myself today. G. K. CHESTERTON

Swans sing before they die – 'twere no bad thing
Should certain persons die before they sing. S. T. COLERIDGE

The Dodo never had a chance. He seems to have been invented for the sole purpose of becoming extinct.
WILL CUPPY

If we were not perfectly convinced that Hamlet's father died before the play began, there would be nothing remarkable about his taking a stroll at night upon his own ramparts.
CHARLES DICKENS

Self-decapitation is an extremely difficult, not to say dangerous, thing to attempt. W. S. GILBERT

The man recovered of the bite,
  The dog it was that died. OLIVER GOLDSMITH

If all dead people had tombs like that of King Cheops, the living would barely have standing room on the earth.
LAMBERT JEFFRIES

I detest life-insurance agents: they always argue that I shall die some day, which is not so. STEPHEN LEACOCK

Die, Doctor? That's the last thing I shall do!
LORD PALMERSTON (last words, attributed)

Waldo is one of those people who would be enormously improved by death. SAKI

I am dying, as I have lived, beyond my means. OSCAR WILDE

There were no last words. His wife was with him to the end.
ANON

DENTISTS – *see also* DOCTORS.
A dentist is a prestidigitator who puts metal in your mouth and pulls coins out of your pocket. AMBROSE BIERCE

I am trying to answer, mouth full of junk, a polite question ...
How difficult it is to steer the words round probes, forceps,
wadding, drills, and that water thing! ARTHUR MARSHALL

I detest everything about the twentieth century except its
dentistry. A. L. ROWSE

"If you've been here six weeks, and mine was your first tooth,
the practice can't be very large." GEORGE BERNARD SHAW

All dentists talk while they work. They have inherited this
from their professional ancestors, the barbers. MARK TWAIN

"It's vulgar to talk like a dentist when one isn't a dentist. It
produces a false impression." OSCAR WILDE

DOCTORS – *see also* DENTISTS, HOSPITALS, ILLNESS.
"He's sent people to their graves, convinced they were
critically ill, when in fact they were perfectly fit. He's
pronounced people A-One, and they've dropped dead in his
waiting-room on the way out." ALAN AYCKBOURN

Physicians of the Utmost Fame
Were called at once; but when they came
They answered, as they took their Fees,
"There is no Cure for this Disease". HILAIRE BELLOC

At a medical conference they naturally provide a hall for a
few enthusiasts to hear one another rambling away over some
cracked lantern slides shown upside down. The rest of the
doctors take the chance to clear off and play golf.
RICHARD GORDON

The consultant physicians and surgeons could easily be
picked out, for they always moved from one spot to another

in public as if they were in a desperate hurry.
RICHARD GORDON

People often say to me, "Vets must know just as much as doctors," but when it comes to the crunch they are never very keen to let me treat them. JAMES HERRIOT

When I was young and full of life
I loved the local doctor's wife,
And ate an apple every day
To keep the doctor far away. THOMAS LAMONT

A man who can read a doctor's prescription written with a post-office pen is a magician. GEORGE McATHY

The best doctors in the world are Dr Diet, Dr Quiet, and Dr Merryman. JONATHAN SWIFT (1667–1745)

He wrote a doctor's hand – the hand which from the beginning of time has been so disastrous to the pharmacist and so profitable to the undertaker. MARK TWAIN

DREAMS – *see also* BED, SLEEP.
Macaulay... dreamt that after he had used Pepys's diary extensively, his small niece confessed to having forged the whole thing. ARTHUR BRYANT

There is a gnomic Japanese tale about a prince who dreamt he was a butterfly, and when he woke up could not be certain that he was not a butterfly dreaming he was a prince.
ALAN COREN

Dreams are, of course, tremendously significant, and, *if dreamt properly*, and subsequently analysed properly, should at once reveal your normal hatred of your mother.
W. C. SELLAR & R. J. YEATMAN

DRINKING – *see also* EATING.
If all be true as I do think,
There are Five Reasons we should drink:
Good Wine, a Friend, or being dry,
Or lest we should be by and by –
Or any other Reason why. HENRY ALDRICH (1647–1710)

Abstainer: a weak person who yields to the temptation of denying himself a pleasure. AMBROSE BIERCE

I keep all my drinks in the bottom of the sideboard, and I can't get at them till I've asked the fattest guest to get out of the armchair I've just put him in. J. BASIL BOOTHROYD

A Bloody Mary is like food, thick and creamy, almost choking you like a swollen tongue, the quickest breakfast Kelloggs never made. ALAN BRIEN

Drink because you are happy, never because you are miserable. G. K. CHESTERTON

Came home at 3.15, not tight, loosened, if anything, one or two joints unbolted, no more than that, perfectly capable of sticking key in letter-box and walking into Christmas tree.
ALAN COREN

And Noah he often said to his wife when he sat down to dine, "I don't care where the water goes if it doesn't get into the wine." G. K. CHESTERTON

No animal ever invented anything as bad as drunkenness – or as good as drink. G. K. CHESTERTON

It was Mr Western's custom every afternoon, as soon as he was drunk, to hear his daughter play on the harpsichord, for he was a great lover of music. HENRY FIELDING

I never drink anything stronger than gin before breakfast. W. C. FIELDS

Take counsel in wine, but resolve afterwards in water. BENJAMIN FRANKLIN

No New Yorker has tasted a drink in his life, all refreshments being served cold enough immediately to paralyse the taste-buds. RICHARD GORDON

He hasn't yet found out how much drink he can hold ... His high-water mark for beer is somewhere in his boots. IAN HAY

The wine is full of gases,
    Which are to me offensive;
It pleases all you asses
    Because it is expensive. A. P. HERBERT

For any ceremonial purpose the otherwise excellent liquid, water, is unsuitable in colour and other respects. A. P. HERBERT

He finished his half-pint ... with the slowness of a man unable to see where the next was coming from. W. W. JACOBS

I heard a man, going up a mountain in Switzerland, say he'd give worlds for a glass of beer, and when he came to a little shanty where they kept it, he kicked up a most fearful row

because they charged him five francs for a bottle of Bass.
J. K. JEROME

For my taste, no cup of tea can be too large. C. S. LEWIS

The distillery had failed because of the owner's sentimental
attachment to his own wares. He could not bear the thought
of other people drinking the precious fluid. A. G. MACDONELL

Their idea of a celebration is to go to a pub and drink six
beers. W. SOMERSET MAUGHAM

The Swiss love to pour a little cognac into everything... At a
dinner I attended in Lausanne an Englishman tasted so much
brandy in the soup that he lifted his plate of consommé and
declared solemnly: "Ladies and gentlemen – the King!"
GEORGE MIKES

The wine flowed like water; towards the end of the evening it
tasted like it. SPIKE MILLIGAN

Two inches to the north-west is written a word full of
meaning – the most purposeful word that can be written on a
map. "Inn." A. A. MILNE

Drink is a serious problem, particularly on cricket tours, for
it can be said without fear of contradiction that nothing yet
devised by man is worse for a sick hangover than a day's
cricket in the summer sun. MICHAEL PARKINSON

There are two reasons for drinking: one is, when you are
thirsty, to cure it; the other, when you are not thirsty, to
prevent it. T. L. PEACOCK

They never taste, who always drink.
MATTHEW PRIOR (1664–1721)

James Watt spent all that time watching the kettle boil. and

the least he could have done was to invent the tea-bag.
OLIVER PRITCHETT

"I'm only a beer teetotaller, not a champagne teetotaller."
GEORGE BERNARD SHAW

Wine is the juice of the grape gone bad. LORD SOPER

An old saying and a true – "much drinking, little thinking".
JONATHAN SWIFT (1667–1745)

Water, taken in moderation, cannot hurt anybody.
MARK TWAIN

Alcohol increases a mild gloom while creating the illusion of
numbing it. A. N. WILSON

All animals are strictly dry:
They sinless live, and swiftly die.
But sinful, ginful, rum-soaked men
Survive for threescore years and ten;
And some, as anyone can see,
Stay pickled till they're ninety-three. ANON

Because it is *de rigueur* at a wine tasting to roll your drink

around your mouth... and then spit it out into a bin of
sawdust, there is no need to do the same with your dry
Martini at a reception. B. A. YOUNG

DROWNING – *see also* BOATS, SEASIDE.
I've always thought the worst thing about drowning was
having to call "Help!" You must look such a fool. It's put me
against drowning. J. BASIL BOOTHROYD

"I am a demd villain! I will fill my pockets with change for a
sovereign in half-pence and drown myself in the Thames!"
CHARLES DICKENS

DUELLING – *see also* ENEMY.
"Thinking men have condemned the duel, and laws have
prohibited it . . . If a man calls upon me with a challenge in his
hand I knock him down." H. H. BRACKENRIDGE

If I thought he had been valiant and so cunning in fence I'd
have seen him damned ere I challenged him.
WILLIAM SHAKESPEARE *(Twelfth Night)*

I think I could wipe out a dishonour by crippling the other
man, but I don't see how I could do it by letting him cripple
me. MARK TWAIN

The modern French duel is... one of the most dangerous
institutions of our day. Since it is nearly always fought in the
open air, the contestants are nearly sure to catch cold.
MARK TWAIN

EATING – *see also* COOKING, DRINKING.
A fork is an instrument used chiefly for the purpose of putting
dead animals into the mouth. AMBROSE BIERCE

He said he was completely off his appetite. As he said this he had his second helping of a heaped-up plate of roast goose, after a plentiful dish of fried sole. After the goose there was just a soupçon of cold tongue and ham, and then came a beautifully done soufflé. Cheese, of course. (Rt. Hon. Henry Chaplin, M.P.) R. D. BLUMENFELD

After dinner sit a while; after supper walk a mile.
WILLIAM CAMDEN (1551–1623)

English people occasionally go a bit red in the face when they have been kept waiting three quarters of an hour for lunch and are then told that everything is off except cottage pie.
HENRY CECIL

The menu was written in a sort of super-French employed by cooks, but quite unintelligible to Frenchmen.
G. K. CHESTERTON

His wife slipped the evening meal into his hand – a packet of frozen soup. "Hurry and eat it," she said, "before it thaws."
JONATHAN CLEMENTS

English puddings are eaten to keep out the cold.
LEN DEIGHTON

"I feel a very unusual sensation," said Mr St. Barbe, after dining. "If it's not indigestion, I think it must be gratitude."
BENJAMIN DISRAELI

Accidents will happen, such as spilling soup down a diner's neck. If the waiter is wise he will not attempt to apologize. He will disappear instantly. PAUL EDWARDS

The waiter should bring in a small dish of olives exactly as if he were carrying John the Baptist's head on a charger.
PAUL EDWARDS

A Lord Chancellor at lunch at his club ... began with half the upper side of an enormous *Turbot au Gratin*. Then he had two immense beef-steaks, the greater part of an apple-pie, at least a quarter of a pound of Stilton, and some grilled herring-roes on toast ... I don't know what he had for dinner.
FORD MADOX FORD

Things that are said to do one good generally taste of sawdust and burnt rubber. R. W. B. HOWARTH

The French market-stalls charge you for what you are going to eat; the English for what you will have to throw away.
SPIKE HUGHES

If you are ever at a loss to support a flagging conversation, introduce the subject of eating. LEIGH HUNT

We never *eat* anybody's health, always *drink* it. Why should we not stand up now and then and eat a tart to somebody's success? J. K. JEROME

I had a tame rat when I was a boy... and one day it fell into a large dish of gooseberry-fool that was standing to cool in the kitchen. Nobody knew what had happened to the poor creature, until the second helping. J. K. JEROME

He who does not mind his belly will hardly mind anything else. SAMUEL JOHNSON

I saw the Eskimo cast many longing looks at the piece of yellow soap we were using. At length I determined to make him happy, and he devoured it with delight.
G. F. LYON (1824)

We may live without poetry, music, and art;
We may live without conscience, and live without heart;
We may live without friends; we may live without books;
But civilized man cannot live without Cooks. LORD LYTTON

I've never really cared for Gutta percha sandwiches and purée of boot polish. LORD MANCROFT (On a cheap flight to New York.)

We asked for a square meal, and they offered us dog biscuits.
JOHN MARSHALL

"I've noticed you always get the best food if you come in unexpectedly and have the same as they're having in the servants' hall." W. SOMERSET MAUGHAM

On the continent people use a fork as if it were a shovel; in England they turn it upside down and push everything – including peas – on top of it. GEORGE MIKES

The "Leek Soup" tasted like rusty water which had somehow leaked through the ceiling on to the plates. FRANK MUIR

There was only one occasion in my life when I put myself on a strict diet... and it was the most miserable afternoon I've ever spent. DENIS NORDEN

He argued that you cannot hope to elevate the masses until you have brought plovers' eggs into their lives. SAKI

I have been persistently strict in sticking to things that didn't agree with me until one or other got the best of it.
MARK TWAIN

A roll and butter and a small coffee seemed the only things on the menu that hadn't been specially prepared by the nastier-minded members of the Borgia family for people they had a particular grudge against. P. G. WODEHOUSE

A lady living in Shanghai found her Chinese cook cleaning lettuce leaves with a toothbrush. When she censured him he explained reassuringly that he wasn't using *her* toothbrush – he was using his own! *Heard on radio*

ECCENTRICS
I had invited Mr and Mrs Meynell and the poet, Francis Thompson, to come for the night, but Meynell explained that this was impossible, "the poet having an inconvenient habit of setting his bed on fire". WILFRED SCAWEN BLUNT

A woman who wall-papered a public lavatory was among the eighty people who responded to a survey on eccentrics.
JENNY BRYAN

Nothing so endeared George III to his subjects as his characteristic enquiry as to how the apple got into the dumpling. ARTHUR BRYANT

My father still spoke of Almighty God as a junior partner in all his enterprises. R. F. DELDERFIELD

The fact that I was using her one very special beloved and delicately nurtured frying-pan upset the cook so much that she locked herself in the larder with all the food, and we had to make our Sunday dinner off bananas. MONICA DICKENS

Not everyone has the outrageous aplomb of an old friend of mine, born to servants but through financial necessity reduced to answering his own front door. The unwelcome neighbour would receive the politest of smiles and the simple statement: "I am not at home". JUDY FROSHAUG

Robert Bridges, the Poet Laureate, was so convinced that his house would burn down that when the expected finally happened, he merely observed to the cabman who was bringing him home, "Ah, at last! Drive on!"
RICHARD JENKYNS

A Lancing College master one day found a boy pulling the nose of another pupil. He put the offending boy's nose under the lid of a desk and sat on it. G. F. LAMB

I once knew a man who spent half his time tying up his bootlaces under lamp-posts. He had an invincible belief that detectives followed him, and he was never content until he had allowed whoever was behind him to get past.
ROBERT LYND

When I met my first snail-watcher and saw him crawl round on all fours in a friend's garden for hours on end, I thought he was mad. I still do. GEORGE MIKES

He is a strong supporter of Atlantis, that magnificent civilization which disappeared beneath the ocean waves several thousands of years ago, doubtless with an unpleasant gurgling noise. PATRICK MOORE

I have... a Scottish correspondent who spends his leisure

hours collecting the registration numbers of bassoons.
PATRICK MOORE

"The dear Archdeacon is getting so absent-minded. He read a
list of box-holders for the opera as the First Lesson the other
Sunday... Fortunately no one noticed the mistake." SAKI

Mr Michael Nance, of Teignmouth, has built a 25-foot high
replica of the Statue of Liberty in his back garden. "It beats
garden gnomes," he said. *Sunday Telegraph*

An old gentlewoman died here two months ago, and left
money in her will to have eight men and eight maids bearers.
But bearers, parson, and clerk must all be true virgins... So
the poor woman lies still unburied.
JONATHAN SWIFT (1667–1745)

One man, I remember, used to take off his hat and set fire to
his hair every now and then. DYLAN THOMAS

Aunt Sarah never went to bed at night without the fear that a
burglar was going to get in and blow chloroform under her
door through a tube. To avert this calamity... she always
piled her money, silverware, and other valuables in a neat
stack just outside her bedroom, with a note reading: "This is
all I have. Please take it and do not use your chloroform".
JAMES THURBER

He was as short-sighted as the editor who used to rub out with
his nose what he wrote with his pen. MARK TWAIN

Bronson Albery was famous for his extraordinary capacity
for talking to himself at full volume, contradicting himself,
scolding himself, agreeing with himself, and in general
coming out of such arguments moderately well.
PETER USTINOV

Lytton Strachey liked being original, and he made his coffee as the alchemists conducted their experiments, with a series of retorts, a structure of glass tubes, standing on a table. The result was striking; the coffee was cold. J. DOVER WILSON

EDUCATION – *see also* CHILDREN, SCHOOL, TEACHERS, UNIVERSITY.
We were determined to stay ignorant, and the masters had long given up attempting to change our minds. ALAN BRIEN

A primary duty of education is to let curiosity rip.
IVOR BROWN

I am wholly against children wasting their time in the idleness of what is called education. WILLIAM COBBETT

We were involved in the Herculean task of discovering how long it would take six men to build a wall if three of them took a week. I seem to recall that we spent almost as much time on this problem as the men spent on the wall. GERALD DURRELL

Examiners, like lightning, never strike twice in the same place. RICHARD GORDON

I could never understand why a small boy was expected to write verses in Greek, at a time when he could scarcely write his own name in English. PATRICK HASTINGS

The great advantage of the sort of education I had was precisely that it made practically no mark upon those subjected to it. MALCOLM MUGGERIDGE

Nothing that is worth knowing can be taught. OSCAR WILDE

EGOTISM – *see also* SELFISHNESS, SMUGNESS.
Egotist: a person of low taste more interested in himself than in me. AMBROSE BIERCE

I is the most popular letter in the alphabet. OLIVER HERFORD

He fell in love with himself at first sight. ANTHONY POWELL

To love oneself is the beginning of a lifelong romance.
OSCAR WILDE

ENEMY – *see also* **ARMY, DUELLING.**
Sir Matthew spent the morning designing mausoleums for his
enemies. ERIC LINKLATER

There is no stronger bond of friendship than a mutual enemy.
F. FRANKFORT MOORE

ENGLISH – *see also* **FOREIGNERS, FRANCE, IRISH, JEWS,
WALES.**
Mad dogs and Englishmen go out in the midday sun.
NOEL COWARD

"Englishmen think over a compliment for a week, so that by
the time they pay it, it is addled, like a bad egg." W. J. LOCKE

In the time of Richard I the ordinary imprecation of a
Norman gentleman was "May I become an Englishman!"
T. B. MACAULAY

An Englishman, even when he is alone, forms an orderly
queue of one. GEORGE MIKES

Many may wonder how the English acquired their reputation
of not working as hard as most Continentals. I am able to
solve the mystery. They acquired this reputation by not
working as hard. GEORGE MIKES

The Englishman's right to walk under the wheels of lorries
was secured in Magna Carta. GEORGE MIKES

A man in a queue is as much the image of a true Briton as a man in a bull-ring is the image of a Spaniard. GEORGE MIKES

The English eat a great deal at Dinner; they rest awhile, then to it again, till they have quite stuffed their paunch. HENRI MISSON (late 17th century)

An Englishman across the aisle [of the railway compartment] did an extraordinary thing, for an Englishman. He asked me a question. PAUL THEROUX

Most Englishmen have the soul of a butler in them. After all, it is a chance to serve. PETER TOWNSEND

EPITAPHS – *see also* DEATH.
Beneath this mound Charles Crocker now reposes;
Step lightly, strangers – also hold your noses.
AMBROSE BIERCE

Here lies my wife: so let her lie!
Now she's at rest, and so am I! JOHN DRYDEN

Here lies, bowled out by Death's unerring ball,

A Cricketer renowned, by name John Small.
But though his name was Small, yet great his fame,
For nobly did he play the noble game.
PIERCE EGAN (On a famous Hambledon player, 1737–1826)

Under this stone, reader, survey
Dead John Vanbrugh's house of clay.
Lie heavy on him, earth, for he
Laid many heavy loads on thee!
ABEL EVANS (Vanbrugh, dramatist and architect, was
designer of Blenheim Palace, built c. 1705.)

For his own tombstone
Life is a jest, and all things show it.
I thought so once; but now I know it.
JOHN GAY (1685–1732)

I'm Smith of Stoke, aged sixty-odd.
    I've lived without a dame
From youth-time on; and would to God
    My dad had done the same.
THOMAS HARDY (on a Pessimist)

Here lies a young author of no reputation,
Who lived by his pen, and thus died of starvation.
He forwards to Heaven a soul in dejection –
Enclosing a stamp for the usual rejection.
LAMBERT JEFFRIES

As in life so in death lies a bat of renown,
    Slain by a lorry (three ton);
His innings is over, his bat is laid down:
    To the end a poor judge of a run. GEORGE McWILLIAM

Beneath this slab
John Brown is stowed.
He watched the ads
And not the road. OGDEN NASH

Here lie I and my four daughters,
Killed by drinking Cheltenham waters:
Had we stuck to Epsom salts
We wouldn't have been in these here vaults. ANON

Beneath this silent stone is laid
A noisy, talkative old maid,
Whose tongue was only stayed by death,
And ne'er before was out of breath. ANON

This is the grave of Mike O'Day
Who died maintaining his right of way.
His right was clear, his will was strong,
But he's just as dead as if he'd been wrong. ANON

Stranger approach this spot with gravity:
John Birningham is filling his last cavity.
ANON (on a dentist's tomb)

Here lie I by the chancel door;
They put me here because I was poor.
The further in, the more you pay,
But here lie I as snug as they.
ANON (on a Devon tombstone)

Accidentally shot by his orderly. "Well done, thou good and
faithful servant."
ANON (on a memorial stone in North-West India)

Here lies Anne Mann;
She lived an old maid
And died an old Mann. ANON (in Bath Abbey)

EQUALITY – *see also* **ARISTOCRACY, CLASS.**
The idea of taking away property from other people has
much more appeal if one has none of one's own.
DUKE OF EDINBURGH

The claim to equality is made only by those who feel themselves to be in some way inferior. C. S. LEWIS

Equality means that you are just as good as the next man but the next man is not half as good as you are. GEORGE MIKES

All animals are equal, but some are more equal than others. GEORGE ORWELL

ETIQUETTE – *see also* ARISTOCRACY, POLITENESS.
Curtsey while you're thinking what to say. It saves time. LEWIS CARROLL

Proprieties that have gone the way of the bustle, the parasol, and the game of croquet. R. F. DELDERFIELD

He found that a fork in his inexperienced hand was an instrument of chase rather than capture. H. G. WELLS

Etiquette is the noise you don't make while having soup. ANON

EXERCISE – *see also* SPORT, WALKING.
Don Francesco was a fisher of men, and of women... It was his way of taking exercise. NORMAN DOUGLAS

Exercise is a short cut to the cemetery. JOHN MORTIMER

I have never taken any exercise except sleeping and resting. MARK TWAIN

EXPERIENCE
"You will think me lamentably crude; my experience of life has been drawn from life itself." MAX BEERBOHM

Experience is the wisdom that enables us to recognize... the folly that we have already embraced. AMBROSE BIERCE

Experience teaches slowly. J. A. FROUDE

For sterile wearience and drearience
Depend, my boy, upon experience. OGDEN NASH

Experience is the one thing you have plenty of when you're too old to get the job. LAURENCE PETER

Experience is the comb Life gives you after you've lost your hair. JUDITH STERN

EXPLORATION – *see also* TRAVEL.

Begin with a clear idea *which Pole* you are dashing at, and try to start facing the right way. W. C. SELLAR & R. J. YEATMAN

Choose your companions carefully; you may have to eat them. W. C. SELLAR & R. J. YEATMAN

FACE – *see also* **BEARDS, BEAUTY, BODY, HAIR.**
A white-flecked auburn moustache dangled like a bunch of radishes beneath his nose. KENNETH ALLSOP

My face looks like a wedding-cake that has been left out in the rain. W. H. AUDEN

Not even a moustache has ever come between my nose and me. JIMMY DURANTE

A beneficent providence has dimmed my powers of sight, so that at a distance of more than four or five yards I am blissfully unaware of the full horror of the average human countenance. ALDOUS HUXLEY

The eyes are the silent orators of the mind. Like all orators, they are apt to deceive. LAMBERT JEFFRIES

He opened his eyes with a sound like the tearing apart of fly-papers. SPIKE MILLIGAN

His eyes were so close together that to look left or right one of them appeared to cross the bridge of his nose.
SPIKE MILLIGAN

Be true to your teeth lest your teeth be false to you.
DEREK ROY

The first time I noticed the double chin I was really scared. For several weeks I did exercises night and morning, hopping and slapping exercises ... but the only result was a third chin to join the others. G. W. STONIER

A face like a carving abandoned as altogether too unpromising for completion. H. G. WELLS

Her mouth had the coldly forbidding look of the closed door

of a subway express when you have just missed the train.
P. G. WODEHOUSE

FASHION – *see also* CLOTHES.
How apt fashionable men are to be fond of slang diction.
GEORGE DARLEY

The surest way to be out of fashion tomorrow is to be in the forefront of it today. DEREK MARLOWE

Women's styles may change, but their designs remain the same. OSCAR WILDE

FISH – *see also* ANIMALS, BIRDS, CATS AND DOGS, HORSE, INSECTS.
"Will you walk a little faster," said a whiting to a snail,
"There's a porpoise close behind us, and he's treading on my tail." LEWIS CARROLL

Beware as you get the octopus on board. Suddenly he relaxes his grasp, and shoots out a jet of ink, which smarts considerably. WILFRED GRENFELL

A friend of ours, who is an admirer of Isaac Walton, was struck, just as we were, with the likeness of the old angler's face to a fish. LEIGH HUNT

We really cannot see what equanimity there is in jerking a lacerated carp out of the water by the jaws, merely because it has not the power of making a noise; for we presume that the most philosophic of anglers would hardly delight in catching a shrieking fish. LEIGH HUNT

The herring is a lucky fish
　　From all disease inured;
Should he be ill while caught at sea,
　　Immediately – he's cured! SPIKE MILLIGAN

Enjoy thy stream, O harmless fish;
And when an angler for his dish,
　　Through gluttony's vile sin,
Attempts, the wretch, to pull thee *out*,
God give thee strength, O gentle trout,
　　To pull the rascal *in*! JOHN WOLCOT

FLATTERY – *see also* HONESTY, TRUTH.
Flattery never seems absurd;
The flattered always take your word. JOHN GAY (1685–1732)

Women hate flattery, so they tell you; and when you say, "Ah, darling, it isn't flattery in your case, it's plain sober truth"... they will smile a quiet approving smile.
J. K. JEROME

"What really flatters a man is that you think him worth flattering." GEORGE BERNARD SHAW

'Tis an old maxim in the schools
That flattery's the food of fools;
But now and then your men of wit
Will condescend to take a bit.
JONATHAN SWIFT (1667–1745)

FLYING – *see also* MOTORING, TRAVEL.
At a meeting held last night in the R.A.F. mess, Prangmere, many witnesses gave their views on a topic of outstanding interest... just how does a fly land on the ceiling?
ANTHONY ARMSTRONG

There was a *Punch* joke about a caterpillar saying to a butterfly, "You'll never get *me* up in one of those things!"
J. BASIL BOOTHROYD

There's nothing like an airport for bringing you down to earth. RICHARD GORDON

FOREIGNERS – *see also* ENGLISH, FRANCE, IRISH, JEWS, WALES.

The highest compliment that can be paid to a foreigner is to be stopped in the street and asked the way by a native.
E. V. LUCAS

"Abroad is unutterably bloody and foreigners are fiends."
NANCY MITFORD

My father always felt perfectly at home there because he never attempted to talk to or make friends with the natives.
ROBERT MORLEY

FORESIGHT

Foresight is the spending of fifty years of adult life in comparative drudgery in order to be able to spend the remaining ten in a nursing home. LAMBERT JEFFRIES

FORTUNE-TELLING – *see also* PROPHECY.

How happy are astrologers, who are believed if they tell one truth to a hundred lies, while other people lose all credit if they tell one lie to a hundred truths.
FRANCESCO GUICCIARDINI (16th century)

If the Delphic priestess was visited by a king or general about to do battle, she was likely to say that a great army was destined to suffer defeat; and unless both sides ran away, it usually did. E. V. KNOX

Whom shall I marry? How much money shall I have?...
These are the questions to which professional fortune-tellers
have long since learned to design satisfactory answers.
ERIC RUSSELL

The fault, dear Brutus, is not in our stars but in ourselves.
WILLIAM SHAKESPEARE *(Julius Caesar)*

[Fortune-tellers] existed to sustain their clients' optimism.
When Anne Boleyn was pregnant, it was no accident that all
the contemporary wizards predicted that the child she bore
Henry VIII would be a son. KEITH THOMAS

FRANCE – *see also* **ENGLISH, FOREIGNERS, IRISH, JEWS,
WALES.**
How can you be expected to govern a country that has 246
different kinds of cheese? CHARLES de GAULLE

Summoning all her courage, Mother would display her
complete mastery over the French tongue. *"Oui, oui!"* she
would exclaim, smiling nervously. GERALD DURRELL

It's always a mistake trying to speak French to the Frogs. As
Noel Coward once remarked when he was sustaining a role at
the Comédie Française, "They don't understand their own
language." ROBERT MORLEY

France has for centuries blocked our way to Europe. Before
the invention of the aeroplane we had to step over it to get
anywhere. ROBERT MORLEY

FREEDOM
Freedom is the right to tell people what they do not want to
hear. GEORGE ORWELL

It was only after our great war for freedom (1914–18), and to make the world safe for democracy, that we were all clamped into the passport system. J. B. PRIESTLEY

Liberty doesn't work as well in practice as it does in speeches. WILL ROGERS

"Englishmen never will be slaves: they are free to do whatever the Government and public opinion allow them to do." GEORGE BERNARD SHAW

Man is *not* born free; he is born attached to his mother by a cord and is incapable of looking after himself for at least seven years. KATHERINE WHITEHORN

FRIENDSHIP – *see also* HOSPITALITY.
While your friend holds you affectionately by both your hands, you are safe, for you can watch both his. AMBROSE BIERCE

Of all the plagues, good Heaven, thy wrath can send,
Save me, oh save me, from the candid friend. GEORGE CANNING

An open foe may prove a curse,
But a pretended friend is worse. JOHN GAY (1685–1732)

A friend that isn't in need is a friend indeed. KIN HUBBARD

Money can't buy friends, but you can get a better class of enemy. SPIKE MILLIGAN

Anyone can sympathize with the sufferings of a friend, but it requires a fine nature to sympathize with a friend's success. OSCAR WILDE

FRUSTRATION – *see also* PESSIMISM, TYRE.

Even when I put my Sunray lamp on, it rains on me.
WOODY ALLEN

I have discovered a law which states that the information
you particularly need is on the only piece of paper you
cannot find. JANE IONS

Why is it that when I have a cup of tea in one hand and a plate
of sticky cakes in the other, I invariably want to sneeze?
LAMBERT JEFFRIES

I never had a piece of toast
Particularly long and wide,
But fell upon the sanded floor,
And always on the buttered side. JAMES PAYN

FUNERALS – *see also* CHURCH, DEATH.
"If you don't go to other men's funerals they won't go to
yours." CLARENCE DAY

As grand and griefless as a rich man's funeral.
SYDNEY DOBELL

He was a broken-down clergyman. Drink had been his
trouble. He had ended by arriving at a funeral in a very
hilarious state, and falling into the grave. RUSSELL NADIN

"They do say," said Uncle Pentstemon, "one funeral makes many." H. G. WELLS

FUTURE
You can never plan the future by the past. EDMUND BURKE

This is the first age that has paid much attention to the future, which is rather ironic since we may not have one.
ARTHUR C. CLARKE

The future is something which everyone reaches at the rate of sixty minutes an hour. C. S. LEWIS

The best thing about the future is that it comes only one day at a time. ABRAHAM LINCOLN

There's a good time coming, boys,
  A good time coming. CHARLES MACKAY

"Time enough to think of the future when you haven't any future to think of." GEORGE BERNARD SHAW

GAMBLING – *see also* CARDS, RACING.

Henry VIII lost the bells of St Paul's in a dice game.
MARCEL BERLINS

The urge to gamble is so universal and its practice so pleasurable that I assume it must be evil. HEYWOOD BROUN

For most men (till by losing rendered sager)
Will back their own opinions by a wager. LORD BYRON

If you can make a heap of all your winnings
And risk it on one turn of pitch-and-toss...
     You'll be an ass, my son. LAMBERT JEFFRIES

The race is not always to the swift, nor the battle to the strong
– but that's the way to bet. DAMON RUNYON

There are two occasions in a man's life when he shouldn't bet: when he can't afford it, and when he can. MARK TWAIN

Gentlemen whose carriages roll upon the four aces are apt to have a wheel out of order. JOHN VANBRUGH (1664–1726)

GAMES – *see also* **CRICKET, RACING, SPORT, TENNIS.**
I thought the idea of the game (American football) was to run head first into the other players and the ball was only there as a sop. CLEMENT FREUD

Well, I won one game in a row.
VICTOR KORCHNOI (Chess master)

Almost any game with any ball is a good game. ROBERT LYND

That Chess was invented by a woman is obvious, for why else should the Queen be the most powerful piece of them all?
A. A. MILNE

Any golfer whose ball hits a seagull shall be said to have scored a "birdie". FRANK MUIR

David Bronstein, a Soviet chess champion in the early 1950s,

once spent fifty minutes studying his *first* move.
Reader's Digest

GARDENING
I value my garden more for being full of blackbirds than of
cherries. JOSEPH ADDISON (1672–1719)

Of every single garden pest
I think I hate the greenfly best. REGINALD ARKELL

The kind of grass I've got in the garden lies down under the
mower and pops up again as soon as it's passed.
J. BASIL BOOTHROYD

Unkempt about those hedges blows
An English unofficial rose. RUPERT BROOKE

A weed is a plant whose virtues have not yet been discovered.
R. W. EMERSON

In my father's view plants, like children, should do exactly
what they were told. BUSTER LLOYD-JONES

My garden will never make me famous;
I'm a gardening ignoramus. OGDEN NASH

One of the most pleasing sounds of Springtime, to be heard
all over the country, is the contented cooing of osteopaths as
Man picks up his garden spade. OLIVER PRITCHETT

GENIUS
Genius has been defined as a supreme capacity for taking
trouble... It might more fitly be described as a supreme
capacity for getting its possessor *into* trouble.
SAMUEL BUTLER

Genius is the capacity for evading hard work.
ELBERT HUBBARD

I have nothing to declare – except my genius.
OSCAR WILDE (at New York Custom House)

HAIR – *see also* **BEARDS, BODY, FACE.**
Charles I, an indolent fellow, found it more convenient to let
his hair grow than to wash his neck. AMBROSE BIERCE

If one really objects to the conversation of barbers, there is
one method of escape which I can easily recommend... that
is, to do all the talking yourself. G. K. CHESTERTON

Years of sorrow and of care
Have made his head come through his hair. HARRY GRAHAM

It was the age when men preferred to shave their heads close
to the scalp and wear a wig. Very sensible, really. It must have
been a great deal easier to take your hair off to look for lice
rather than play hide and seek with something you could not
see. JOHN HEARSEY

Everybody knows what a man's head looks like after a
woman cuts his hair. O. HENRY

There is nothing more contemptible than a bald man who
pretends to have hair. MARTIAL (c.40–104 A.D.)

A cascade of golden hair shook itself loose and fell down
behind, descending to almost as far as where the back
changes its name. DENIS NORDEN

Philip of Macedon made a man a judge. Finding later that the
man's hair and beard were dyed, he removed him, saying, "I
cannot think that a man who is faithless in his hair can be
trusty in his deeds." PLUTARCH (c. 46–120 A.D.)

"A little misery wouldn't matter very much with her; it would go so well with the way she does her hair." SAKI

HEAVEN – *see also* CHURCH, RELIGION.
People who think they are going there often wonder what they will do with themselves in Heaven. J. B. PRIESTLEY

If you go to Heaven without being naturally qualified for it you will not enjoy yourself there. GEORGE BERNARD SHAW

Let us swear while we may, for in Heaven it will not be allowed. MARK TWAIN

HISTORY
History is an account, mostly false, of events, mostly unimportant, which are brought about by rulers, mostly knaves, and soldiers, mostly fools. AMBROSE BIERCE

If I want to get anything out of an antique hunk of masonry lying in the middle of a field with a chain round it, I have to shut my eyes, and tell myself, very slowly and emphatically... "This – is – a very, very old piece of stone, and it's terribly fascinating and marvellous." J. BASIL BOOTHROYD

People flock to Stonehenge on fine week-ends, pay their money, take a good, long, meaningless look, and drive off leaving a lot of orange peel and coke cans, after the manner of culture seekers the world over. J. BASIL BOOTHROYD

It was the Puritans who put an end to the practice of dancing, as well as discontinuing the tradition of kings wearing heads on their shoulders. MIKE HARDING

The first date in English history is 55 B.C. . . . Julius Caesar was compelled to invade Britain again the following year

(54 B.C., not 56, owing to the peculiar Roman method of counting). W. C. SELLAR & R. J. YEATMAN

History is a record of events that didn't happen – made by someone who wasn't there. ANON

HOLIDAYS – *see also* BOATS, HOTELS, SEASIDE.
Arthur Watts (illustrator) kept asking me to "look more dejected". As if, he explained, I was *really* having a holiday with my family. E. M. DELAFIELD

The drawback of all seaside places is that half the landscape is unavailable... being covered with useless water.
NORMAN DOUGLAS

"No holiday is ever anything but a disappointment."
ALDOUS HUXLEY

A period of activity so intense that it can only be undertaken three or four weeks in the year. MILES KINGTON

HONESTY – *see also* LYING, TRUTH.
"It's discouraging to think how many people are shocked by honesty and how few by deceit." NOEL COWARD

"Frank and explicit" – that is the right line to take when you wish to conceal your own mind and to confuse the minds of others. BENJAMIN DISRAELI

Always be sincere, whether you mean it or not.
MICHAEL FLANDERS

Whenever I buy a few things abroad, I hand over a list of my newly acquired goods to the customs official. As so much honesty is much too suspicious, I usually end up by unpacking my whole suitcase. GEORGE MIKES

We must make the world honest before we can honestly say to our children that honesty is the best policy. GEORGE BERNARD SHAW

Honesty is the best policy; but he who acts on that policy is not an honest man. BISHOP WHATELY

HORSE – *see also* ANIMALS, BIRDS, CATS AND DOGS, FISH, HUNTING, INSECTS, RACING.
Oh wasn't it naughty of Smudges?
Oh, Mummy, I'm sick with disgust.
She threw me in front of the judges,
And my silly old collar-bone's bust. JOHN BETJEMAN

Never ride your horse more than five-and-thirty miles a day, always taking more care of him than of yourself; which is right and reasonable, seeing as how the horse is the best animal of the two. GEORGE BORROW

The only trouble with that horse is that it doesn't like jockeys. Once it's thrown its jockey it goes like the wind. HENRY CECIL

A horse which stops dead just before a jump and thus propels its rider into a graceful arc provides a splendid excuse for general merriment. DUKE OF EDINBURGH

A horse is dangerous at both ends and uncomfortable in the middle. IAN FLEMING

I prefer a bike to a horse. The brakes are more easily checked. LAMBERT JEFFRIES

He flung himself on his horse and rode off madly in all directions. STEPHEN LEACOCK

A horse's eye disquiets me: it has an expression of alarm that may at any moment be translated into action. E. V. LUCAS

No garden that boasted geraniums was safe from Ajax's moody munchings. The only time that Madge ever coaxed it as far as Exeter, Ajax ate the whole of a rather elaborate display in the Cathedral Close. ARTHUR MARSHALL

On horseback he seemed to require as many hands as a Hindu god, at least four for clutching the reins, and two more for patting the horse soothingly on the neck. SAKI

We attended stables, as we attended church, in our best clothes, thereby no doubt showing the degree of respect due to horses. OSBERT SITWELL

The steed bit his master.
How came this to pass?
He heard the good pastor
Cry, "All flesh is grass". ANON

There are two important rules in horse-riding. The first is to mount the horse. The second is to stay mounted. ANON

HOSPITALITY – *see also* **FRIENDSHIP**.
Macbeth and Lady Macbeth stand out as the supreme type of all that a host and hostess should not be. MAX BEERBOHM

Hospitality is the virtue which induces us to feed and lodge certain persons who are not in need of food and lodging. AMBROSE BIERCE

HOSPITALS – *see also* **ACCIDENTS, DOCTORS, ILLNESS**.
In the wards the patients are all ill: in out-patients' they are nearly all healthy. RICHARD GORDON

I had never seen a Sister close to before. This unexpected proximity had the effect of being in a rowing-boat under the bows of the *Queen Mary*. RICHARD GORDON

I hastened over to the Orthopaedic Ward, hoping to find the man who knew more about surgical procedures than anyone else in the hospital. Luckily he was still in his Porter's Cubicle. DENIS NORDEN

HOTELS – *see also* HOLIDAYS.

This is a thing which often annoys me about hotels. You walk in, all smiles and anticipation, and there isn't a soul to be seen: proprietor, manager, receptionist, or the man who hopes he won't be asked to take up your luggage. J. BASIL BOOTHROYD

British hotels prefer you to write Mr and Mrs even if you are sinning. LEN DEIGHTON

In the evening there was a dinner at a West End hotel. I am never happy in luxury hotels – it is all those servants creeping around, calling you "Sir" and secretly hating your guts. It cost two shillings to use the toilet. MICHAEL GREEN

[To make tea in the bedroom] you have... to mix together a plastic envelope containing too much sugar, a small plastic pot of something which is not milk but has curdled anyway, and a thin brown packet seemingly containing the ashes of a cremated mole. FRANK MUIR

HOUSE AND HOME – *see also* ARCHITECTURE, HOUSE-WORK.

It is quite cosy in the living-room. After a while I can even remove my overcoat. BRIAN ALDISS

You think you'll do some little job, perfectly simple... Fate isn't going to have it. I once sat down to put some new cotton wool in a cigarette lighter, and before I'd finished I'd got all the floorboards up in the spare bedroom.
J. BASIL BOOTHROYD

Wanted, small guillotine, for home use only.
Chichester Observer (advertisement)

"Mature" means either tumbledown or overgrown, depending on whether it refers to the building or the garden.
PETER CLAYTON

Private guide to estate agents' jargon . . .

Attractive older-style property	A wreck
Cottage-style home	A wreck in a terrace
Town house	A modern wreck in a terrace

MICHAEL GREEN

A dense mass of undergrowth (was) spilling over the pavement. The house was concealed behind this and a privet hedge nine feet tall. We had some difficulty finding the gate and then had literally to hack our way to the front door, which was defended by 49 empty milk bottles. "As you will see, sir," (said the house agent), "there is a lovely mature garden." MICHAEL GREEN

He advised that the privy should in every house be the room nearest to Heaven. ALDOUS HUXLEY

When I put something in a safe place, it simply means that I am not going to see it again for years. MARY KENNY

HOUSEWORK – *see also* **HOUSE AND HOME**.
The trouble about housework is that whatever you do seems to lead to another job to do or a mess to clear up.
MONICA DICKENS

It's a curious fact that good glass cracks at a touch while cheap stuff can be hurled about with perfect safety.
MONICA DICKENS

A clothes line will only snap if the ground beneath it is muddy. FAITH HINES & PAM BROWN

If I were asked to enumerate the Seven Deadly Virtues, the one I'd put at the top of my list . . . is Female Tidiness.
DENIS NORDEN

HUMOUR
The marvellous thing about a joke with a double meaning is that it can mean onlv one thing. RONNIE BARKER

Laughter is a convulsive action of the diaphragm. In this state the person draws a full breath and throws it out in inter-rupted, short, and audible cachinnations.
PROFESSOR CHARLES BELL

The man who cannot laugh is not only fit for treasons, stratagems, and spoils; his whole life is already a treason and a strategem. THOMAS CARLYLE

If Racine knew any jokes, he kept them to himself.
ARTHUR MARSHALL

Everything is funny as long as it happens to someone else.
WILL ROGERS

She has a laugh so hearty it knocks the whipped cream off an order of strawberry shortcake on a table fifty feet away. DAMON RUNYON

"I don't suppose angels have any sense of humour; it would be of no use to them as they never hear any jokes." SAKI

A Scotsman told that it required a surgical operation to get a joke into a Scotsman's head, asked with a puzzled frown, "And why should you wish to get it in?" *Strand Magazine*

Humour is like a frog; if you dissect it, it dies. MARK TWAIN

I am at a loss to understand what can be got out of laughter except loss of dignity. KING WILLIAM III (1650–1702)

The difference between wit and humour beats me, and always has beat me. Sometimes I think I've got it, and then suddenly everything goes black. P. G. WODEHOUSE

Honoria is one of those robust dynamic girls with ... a laugh like a squadron of cavalry charging over a tin bridge. P. G. WODEHOUSE

HUNTING – *see also* ANIMALS, HORSE.
O I love to hunt the tiger bold,
    With shouting loud and free,
In jungles where the sands of gold
    Border the black Gangee.
But when the tiger turns about
    And takes to hunting me,
That's not so fine – I'd rather shout
    As hunter than huntee. AMBROSE BIERCE

For what were all these country patriots born?
To hunt, and vote, and raise the price of corn. LORD BYRON

A keen sportsman, he excelled in fox-hunting, dog-hunting, pig-killing, bat-catching, and the other pastimes of his class.
STEPHEN LEACOCK

While a street-boy who threw a kitten to a crowd of dogs would be rightly condemned, his counterpart who co-operates in urging on a pack of hounds to tear a stag or a fox to pieces is acclaimed as a promising sportsman.
PATRICK MOORE

If foxes, like women, had a vote, I think they would vote unanimously for the keeping up of fox-hunting.
COLONEL SIR LANCELOT ROLLESTON, M.F.H.

When a man wants to murder a tiger he calls it sport; but when the tiger wants to murder him he calls it ferocity.
GEORGE BERNARD SHAW

It's a fine day: let's go out and kill something. ANON

HUSBANDS AND WIVES – *see also* ADULTERY, BED, LOVE, MARRIAGE.
Being pregnant is a very boring six months... It's an occupational hazard of being a wife. PRINCESS ANNE

An archaeologist is the best husband any woman can have. The older she gets, the more interested he is in her.
AGATHA CHRISTIE

Late last night I killed my wife,
   Stretched her on the parquet flooring;
I was loath to take her life,
   But I *had* to stop her snoring. HARRY GRAHAM

A wife is to thank God her husband has faults ... A husband without faults is a dangerous observer.
MARQUIS OF HALIFAX (1661–1715)

Some cunning men choose fools for their wives, thinking to manage them, but they always fail. SAMUEL JOHNSON

Come to some angry words with my wife about neglecting the keeping of the house clean, I calling her a beggar, and she me a pricklouse, which vexed me. SAMUEL PEPYS (1633–1703)

"A woman seeking a husband is the most unscrupulous of all beasts of prey." GEORGE BERNARD SHAW

IDLENESS – see also BED.
My evenings are given over entirely to sloth. I like sloth, it is so restful. JANE IONS

It is impossible to enjoy idling thoroughly unless one has plenty of work to do. There is no fun in doing nothing when you have nothing to do. J. K. JEROME

We would all be idle if we could. SAMUEL JOHNSON

IGNORANCE – see also KNOWLEDGE, MENTAL DEFICIENCY, STUPIDITY.
Ignoramus: a person unacquainted with certain kinds of knowledge familiar to yourself, and having certain other kinds that you know nothing about. AMBROSE BIERCE

Where ignorance is bliss, disillusionment, when it comes, more than makes up for the bliss. LAMBERT JEFFRIES

Everybody is ignorant, only on different subjects.
WILL ROGERS

ILLNESS – see also DOCTORS, HOSPITALS.
Everyone knows how to get rid of this cold but me.
J. BASIL BOOTHROYD

There are those who divide their lives into two parts – "before my operation" and "since my operation".
CHARLES HILL (Radio Doctor)

Complaints about his indigestion began to play a prominent part in his social conversation, and when a man begins to talk about his indigestion he is headed for disaster.
R. W. B. HOWARTH

I have Bright's disease – and he has mine. S. J. PERELMAN

"There is a bug going around," we tell each other. It conjures up a picture of a rather caddish eight-legged character driving around the place in a sports car, causing trouble wherever he goes. OLIVER PRITCHETT

Never talk about your health. When people say "How are you?" they don't really want to know. NOEL STREATFIELD

A friend assured me that it was policy to "feed a cold and starve a fever". I had both. So I thought it best to feed myself up for the cold, and then keep dark and let the fever starve itself. MARK TWAIN

Did you ever have the measles, and if so how many?
ARTEMAS WARD

IMAGINATION

To treat your facts with imagination is one thing; to imagine your facts is another. JOHN BURROUGHS

"The only places John likes on the Continent are those in which it's only by an effort of the imagination that you can tell you're not in England." W. SOMERSET MAUGHAM

The Right Honourable gentleman is indebted to his memory for his jests, and to his imagination for his facts.
R. B. SHERIDAN (of Henry Dundas, M.P.)

INCOMPETENCE

Henry can't even strike a match.
MARGOT ASQUITH (of her husband, Prime Minister 1908–16)

Edgington tying a bootlace could end up with a broken arm.
SPIKE MILLIGAN

I manage my own affairs with as much care and steady attention and skill as – let us say – a drunken Irish tenor.
J. B. PRIESTLEY

Democracy substitutes election by the incompetent many for appointment by the corrupt few. GEORGE BERNARD SHAW

INSECTS – *see also* ANIMALS, BIRDS, CATS AND DOGS, FISH, HORSE.

Buzz, buzz, buzz, buzz! Busy bee! Busy bee!
Sting if you like, but don't sting me! ARTHUR ASKEY

There was an old man in a tree
Who was horribly bored by a bee. EDWARD LEAR

Thus hath the candle sing'd the moth.
O these deliberate fools!
WILLIAM SHAKESPEARE *(Merchant of Venice)*

So, naturalists observe, a flea
Hath smaller fleas that on him prey;
And these have smaller fleas to bite 'em,
And so proceed *ad infinitum*. JONATHAN SWIFT (1667–1745)

Nothing seems to please a fly so much as to be taken for a currant; and if it can be baked in a cake and palmed off on the unwary, it dies happy. MARK TWAIN

INSULTS – *see also* ABUSE, ANGER, CRITICISM, CURSING.
He could not see a belt without hitting below it.
MARGOT ASQUITH (of Lloyd George)

She has the bear's ethereal grace,
    The bland hyena's laugh,
The footsteps of the elephant,
    The neck of a giraffe. LEWIS CARROLL

A modest little man, with much to be modest about.
WINSTON S. CHURCHILL (of Clement Attlee, attributed)

"She has been an extremely competent actress for well over forty years. In addition she has contrived, with uncanny skill, to sustain a spotless reputation for being the most paralysing, epoch-making, monumental, world-shattering, God-awful bore that ever drew breath." NOEL COWARD

Truth for him was a moving target ... he rarely pierced the outer ring.
HUGH CUDLIPP (of W. R. Hearst, American newspaper proprietor)

He'll believe anything provided it's not in Holy Scripture.
BISHOP DOUGLAS FEAVER (of a fellow bishop)

Like precious stones, his sensible remarks
Derive their value from their scarcity. W. S. GILBERT

"I wonder if she goes to lunch on a broomstick?" he said.
RICHARD GORDON

If I never see that woman again, it's too soon.
GROUCHO MARX

Whenever I call an Englishman rude he takes it as a compliment. GEORGE MIKES

A debate without the honourable member would be like *Hamlet* without the third gravedigger.
Speaker at Oxford Union debate.

She ran the gamut of emotions from A to B.
DOROTHY PARKER (of Katharine Hepburn)

"You're looking nicer than usual," I said, "but that's so easy for you." SAKI

"He's studying to be a gentleman farmer, he told me. I didn't ask if both subjects were compulsory." SAKI

Someone cruelly pointed out in print that I looked like an unmade bed. DYLAN THOMAS

He is an old bore; even the grave yawns for him.
H. BEERBOHM TREE (of Israel Zangwill)

IRISH – *see also* **ENGLISH, FOREIGNERS, FRANCE, JEWS, WALES.**
Take the Blarney Stone. Only the Irish could persuade people to kiss a stone the Norman soldiers had urinated on.
DAVE ALLEN

If it was raining soup, we'd be out with forks.
BRENDAN BEHAN

I don't tell Irish jokes any more. I told one at the club last night and an Irishman came after me with a razor! He would have used it too – if he could have found somewhere to plug it in. TERRY HERBERT

When Irish eyes are smiling, watch your step.
GERALD KERSH

The Irish don't know what they want and are prepared to fight to the death to get it. SIDNEY LITTLEWOOD

Did you hear about the Irish girl who went home and told her mother she was pregnant – and the mother said, "Are you sure it's you?" DENNIS TAYLOR

JEWELLERY – *see also* CLOTHES.
I've never hated a man enough to give him his diamonds back. ZSA ZSA GABOR

Kissing your hand makes you feel good, but a diamond bracelet lasts for ever. ANITA LOOS

"Goodness, what beautiful diamonds!"
"Goodness had nothing to do with it, dearie." MAE WEST

JEWS, – *see also* ENGLISH, FOREIGNERS, FRANCE, IRISH, WALES.
Never call a Jew a Jew unless you can be sure of making him lose his temper by doing so. KINGSLEY AMIS

When Balfour launched his scheme for peopling Palestine with Jewish immigrants, I am credibly informed that he did not know there were Arabs in the country.
DEAN W. R. INGE

I'm not really a Jew. Just Jewish – not the whole hog.
JONATHAN MILLER

"The Jews generally give good value. They make you pay, but they deliver the goods." GEORGE BERNARD SHAW

JOURNALISM – *see also* NEWSPAPERS, WRITING.
You are always making use of new envelopes to send me old material. I suggest you use old envelopes and send me new material. LORD BEAVERBROOK

Never again would I give an interview to the London Press . . . Henceforward my views on Birth Control, Television, Long Skirts, D. H. Lawrence, Free Love, and Bicycling Waitresses should be locked in my own bosom. NOEL COWARD

"Anything interesting in *The Times*?"
"Don't be silly, Charles." NOEL COWARD

The hardest-worked word in my vocabulary was "alleged". It can steer you through a mile of rapids. R. F. DELDERFIELD

The news is always bad, even when it sounds good.
ALDOUS HUXLEY

The secret of successful journalism is to make your readers so angry that they are ready to write half your paper for you.
C. E. M. JOAD

Donald Cameron had no qualifications for any profession . . . so he resolved to try his fortune as a journalist.
A. G. MACDONELL

A mixture of arrogance, pomposity, and naïveté is shown by supposedly intelligent men and women who think they have a divine right to go on producing the sort of paper *they* like, irrespective of whether enough people want to read it.
ANGUS MAUDE

When you pay the losses you can say it's your paper too.
RUPERT MURDOCH (to his journalists)

"When once you've seen your features reproduced in the newspaper you feel you would like to be a veiled Turkish woman for the rest of your life." SAKI

You cannot hope to bribe or twist
Thank God! the British journalist.
But seeing what the man will do
Unbribed, there's no occasion to. HUMBERT WOLFE

KICK
It's not really a kick when done by an expert. It's a punch with the foot. JOYCE CARY

KISSING – *see also* LOVE.
In all those games of Postman's Knock I never once remember kissing an open-eyed girl. R. F. DELDERFIELD

If you want to kiss me any time during the evening, just let me know and I'll be glad to arrange it for you. Just mention my name. F. SCOTT FITZGERALD

Kissed her once by the pigsty when she wasn't looking and never kissed her again although she was looking all the time.
DYLAN THOMAS

KNOWLEDGE – *see also* IGNORANCE.
A little knowledge is a dangerous thing, but no knowledge is positively fatal. LAMBERT JEFFRIES

Knowledge advances by steps and not by leaps.
T. B. MACAULAY

It is a great nuisance that knowledge can be acquired only by hard work. W. SOMERSET MAUGHAM

LAW

To appeal, in law, is to put the dice back in the box for another throw. AMBROSE BIERCE

Laws, like houses, lean on one another. EDMUND BURKE

"Here you are, a fully-fledged barrister, licensed to lose anyone's case for him, and you haven't had an hour of practical experience. Now a medical student has to watch a lot of butchery before he qualifies to dig for his first appendix. HENRY CECIL

"Much better" (said Counsel) "to tell you now why you won't win than to explain later why you didn't." HENRY CECIL

Everyone knows the story of the solicitors' corps of volunteers who, when the Colonel on the battlefield cried "Charge!" all said simultaneously, "Six-and-eightpence".
G. K. CHESTERTON (Six shillings and eightpence was formerly the standard solicitor's fee.)

On the whole, barristers are more interested in their briefs than in a girl's. JILLY COOPER

Occasionally a lawyer sends you a legal document covered in kisses, and you really think you're getting somewhere until he tells you he only wants you to sign your name, in three places.
JILLY COOPER

All thieves who could my fees afford
    Relied on my orations,
And many a burglar I've restored
    To his friends and his relations. W. S. GILBERT

My learned profession I'll never disagrace
By taking a fee, with a grin on my face,
When I haven't been there to attend to the case.
W. S. GILBERT

The Common Law of England has been laboriously built up
about a mythical figure – the figure of "the reasonable man".
A. P. HERBERT

An Act of God was defined as "something which no
reasonable man could have expected". A. P. HERBERT

If you want to be let off jury service, the word now goes, turn
up with neat hair and clean, tidy clothes. MARY KENNY

At the top of my street the attorneys abound,
   And down at the bottom the barges are found:
Fly, Honesty, fly to some safer retreat,
   For there's craft in the river, and craft in the street.
JAMES SMITH

LEISURE
"Like every other good thing in this world, leisure and culture
have to be paid for. Fortunately, however, it is not the
leisured and the cultured who have to pay." ALDOUS HUXLEY

LETTERS – *see also* WRITING.
At any given moment in the last few years there have been ten
letters which I absolutely *must* write, thirty which I *ought* to
write, and fifty which any other person in my position *would*
have written. Probably I have written two. A. A. MILNE

I used to look out of my bedroom window every morning to
observe the postman making his tantalising journey down the
street. I do not do that any more because I have discovered

this infallible bit of folk wisdom: "A watched postman never delivers". OLIVER PRITCHETT

LIBRARIES – *see also* **BOOKS, POETRY, PROSE.**
Though universally well spoken of in the cruise literature, ships' libraries aren't wholly to be relied on, partly because of eccentric opening hours, partly because there's often nothing to open but a locked metal bar across a glass-fronted shelf containing five paperbacks. In German.
J. BASIL BOOTHROYD

I've been drunk for about a week ... I thought it might sober me up to sit in a library. F. SCOTT FITZGERALD

We call ourself a rich nation, and we are filthy and foolish enough to thumb each other's books out of circulating libraries. JOHN RUSKIN

"A circulating library in a town is as an evergreen tree of diabolical knowledge. They who are so fond of handling the leaves will long for the fruit at last." R. B. SHERIDAN

LIFE
Life was always like this. Just as something nice and interesting occurred, destiny must intervene with some pressing engagement. CONRAD AIKEN

I take life as it comes, and although I grouse a great deal and sometimes lie on the floor and kick and scream and refuse to eat my supper, I find that taking Life as it comes is the only way to meet it. ROBERT BENCHLEY

Life is rather like a tin of sardines. We are all looking for the key. ALAN BENNETT

The one serious conviction a man should have is that nothing should be taken too seriously. SAMUEL BUTLER

A well-written life is almost as rare as a well-spent one.
THOMAS CARLYLE

Life is a joke that's just begun. W. S. GILBERT

"You will find that at St Swithin's you will learn enough bad habits to make life bearable." RICHARD GORDON

He had decided to live for ever or die in the attempt.
JOSEPH HELLER

Life consists in looking forward and looking backward.
LAMBERT JEFFRIES

Life is a steady walk with a hidden precipice at the end.
LAMBERT JEFFRIES

Truly, there is a tide in the affairs of men; but there is no gulf stream flowing forever in one direction. J. R. LOWELL

On life's vast ocean diversely we sail,
Reason the card, but passion is the gale.
ALEXANDER POPE (1688–1744)

Commuter – one who spends his life
Riding to and from his wife;
A man who shaves, and takes a train,
And then rides back to shave again. E. B. WHITE

LONDON – *see also* ARCHITECTURE, COUNTRYSIDE, WEATHER.
This is Soho, where anything goes, and just make sure it is not your wallet. LEN DEIGHTON

For prisoners in the Tower it was a luxury to be beheaded on Tower Green, for the riff-raff were executed on Tower Hill.
LEN DEIGHTON

You can't get up Nelson's Column unless you're a pigeon.
LEN DEIGHTON

The Gulf Stream, as it nears the shores of the British Isles...
rises into the air, turns into soup, and comes down in
London. STEPHEN LEACOCK

One cannot frequent London restaurants and be utterly
ignorant of Italian. E. V. LUCAS

The Post Office Tower, stacked like a pile of green cotton
reels. A. J. MARSHALL

The air seems so dead in this quiet country . . . I must rush up to London to breathe. GEORGE MEREDITH

Hell is a city much like London –
A populous and smoky city. P. B. SHELLEY

LOVE – *see also* HUSBANDS AND WIVES, KISSING, MARRIAGE, PLATONIC LOVE, SEX.
The test of true love is whether you can endure the thought of cutting your sweetheart's toe-nails. W. N. P. BARBELLION

Love ceases to be a pleasure when it ceases to be a secret. APHRA BEHN (1640–1689)

Men will admire, adore, and die,
While wishing at your Feet they lie;
But admitting their Embraces
Wakes them from the Golden Dream.
WILLIAM CONGREVE (1670–1729)

Would she could make of me a Saint,
  Or I of her a Sinner! WILLIAM CONGREVE

Lapp courtships are conducted pretty much in the same fashion as in other parts of the world. The aspirant, as soon as he discovers he has lost his heart, goes off in search of a friend and a bottle of brandy. LORD DUFFERIN

"I hate all that don't love me, and slight all that do."
GEORGE FARQUHAR (1678–1707)

"He's ugly, and absurdly dressed,
  And sixty-seven nearly,
He's everything that I detest,
But if the truth must be confessed,
  I love him very dearly!" W. S. GILBERT

"What on earth is this love that upsets everybody, and how is it to be distinguished from insanity?" W. S. GILBERT

"Gifted as I am with a beauty that probably no other man on earth can rival... it is my hideous destiny to be madly loved at first sight by every woman I come across." W. S. GILBERT

"I'm engaged to two noblemen at once. That ought to be enough to make any girl happy." W. S. GILBERT

The love of Guido and Isolde was of that pure and almost divine type found only in the Middle Ages. They had never seen one another. They did not know one another.
STEPHEN LEACOCK

"When Gaston proposed to me he went down on his knees, and he took my hand, and said he couldn't live without me. Of course, I knew that, because he hadn't a cent... he'd been haggling with papa for a fortnight about having his debts paid." W. SOMERSET MAUGHAM

"Why didn't you tell me you were going to propose? I'd have had my hair waved." W. SOMERSET MAUGHAM

In the Soviet Union there is no mystical or obscure treatment of love, such as decadent Western poets use. We sing of how a young man falls in love with a girl because of her industrial output. STEPHAN PETROVIV

"Make love in the afternoon... It's the only time for it."
ARNOLD WESKER

When a confirmed bachelor falls in love, he does it with a wholeheartedness beyond the scope of the ordinary man.
P. G. WODEHOUSE

"Grab her, fold her in a close embrace, and hug her till her

ribs squeak. I have tried this policy on several occasions, and I have always found it to give the best results."
P. G. WODEHOUSE

He fell in love, got married ... and then began to find out things. P. G. WODEHOUSE

LYING – *see also* FLATTERY, HONESTY, TRUTH.

If society needed any further proof that the earl was there, the servant persistently asserted that he was not at home.
G. K. CHESTERTON

"How I love thee for that heavenly gift of lying!"
JOHN DRYDEN

"She's too crafty a woman to invent a new lie when an old one will do." W. SOMERSET MAUGHAM

If you can't invent a really convincing lie, it's often better to stick to the truth. ANGELA THIRKELL

MACHINES

I like the way the computer manufacturers call typing on a processor "keystroking", as if you and the machine were meant to have some sort of relationship. JAMES BURKE

Operators at a London technical publications firm were perplexed by the repeated appearance of the phrase "water goat" in the computer translation of their specification. It transpired that what the machine was trying to say was "hydraulic ram". *Daily Telegraph*

I understand that computers store and juggle facts and figures, and are worked either by elastic bands or electricity.
ARTHUR MARSHALL

MARRIAGE – *see also* HUSBANDS AND WIVES, LOVE, SEX.
Even in these days of marital musical chairs many third
fingers still go through life wearing the same old bashed-up
ring. J. BASIL BOOTHROYD

Marriage is the result of a longing for the deep, deep peace of
the double bed after the hurly-burly of the chaise-longue.
MRS.PATRICK CAMPBELL (attributed)

"Let us be as strange (aloof) as if we had been married a great
while; and as well-bred as if we were not married at all."
WILLIAM CONGREVE (1670–1729)

I've sometimes thought of marrying, and then I've thought
again. NOEL COWARD

"We've both been married before – careless rapture at this
stage would be incongruous and embarrassing."
NOEL COWARD

"Nobody but a monumental bore would have thought of
having a honeymoon at Budleigh Salterton." NOEL COWARD

"When you're a married man, Samivel, you'll understand a
good many things as you don't understand now."
CHARLES DICKENS

"If we're weak enough to tarry
    Ere we marry, you and I,
With a more attractive maiden,
    Jewel-laden, you may fly." W. S. GILBERT

"We won't wait long."
"No. We might change our minds. We'll get married first."
"And change our minds afterwards?"
"That's the usual course." W. S. GILBERT

I asked Maureen when she was going to get married, but she

says why buy a book when you can join a circulating library.
MICHAEL GREEN

All marriages are happy. It's the living together afterwards that causes all the trouble. RAYMOND HULL

"All men who get married must 'ave a soft spot somewhere, if it's only in the head." W. W. JACOBS

"If you was a married man, Alf... you wouldn't be surprised at anything." W. W. JACOBS

I believe marriages would in general be as happy, and often more so, if they were all made by the Lord Chancellor, upon a due consideration of characters and circumstances, without the parties having any choice in the matter.
SAMUEL JOHNSON

"Marriages are made in Heaven, and if we once set to work to repair celestial mistakes we shall have our hands full."
HENRY ARTHUR JONES

Before marriage the average man takes little notice of prams. It's only after he's been married for nearly a year that he begins to think as much about prams as he does about cars.
JOHN KENYON

Many a man in love with a dimple makes the mistake of marrying the whole girl. STEPHEN LEACOCK

If a girl desires to woo you, before allowing her to press her suit, ask her if she knows how to press yours.
STEPHEN LEACOCK

Many a promising marriage has foundered in that cold, forbidding gulf between twin beds. JOHN MARSHALL

No matter how happily a woman may be married, it always

pleases her to discover that there is a nice man who wishes she were not. H. L. MENCKEN

Only a married man, with everything in his wife's name, can face with confidence the give and take of the bustling city. A. A. MILNE

"Come, come," said Tom's father, "at your time of life,
There's no longer excuse for thus playing the rake –
It is time you should think, boy, of taking a wife." –
"Why, so it is, father – whose wife shall I take?"
THOMAS MOORE

"Marriage is at best a dangerous experiment." T. L. PEACOCK

Strange to see what delight we married people have to see poor fools decoyed into our condition.
SAMUEL PEPYS (1633–1703)

It doesn't much signify whom one marries, for one is sure to find out next morning that it was someone else.
SAMUEL ROGERS

When a girl marries she exchanges the attentions of many men for the inattention of one. HELEN ROWLAND

Marriage is popular because it combines the maxium of temptation with the maximum of opportunity.
GEORGE BERNARD SHAW

"My mother married a very good man ... and she is not at all keen on my doing the same." GEORGE BERNARD SHAW

When a man marries, dies, or turns Hindoo,
His best friends hear no more of him. P. B. SHELLEY

The reason so few marriages are happy is because young ladies spend their time in making nets, not in making cages. JONATHAN SWIFT (1667–1745)

If people only made prudent marriages, what a stop to population there would be. W. M. THACKERAY

What a fuss there would be if people had to pay the minister as much to marry them as they have to pay a lawyer to get them a divorce. CLAIRE TREVOR

He's the most married man I ever saw in my life. ARTEMUS WARD

"I don't believe," said Mr Prendergast, "that people would ever fall in love or want to be married if they hadn't been told about it. It's like abroad: no one would want to go there if they hadn't been told it existed." EVELYN WAUGH

Marriage is a great institution, but I'm not ready for an institution yet. MAE WEST

"No man should have a secret from his own wife. She invariably finds it out." OSCAR WILDE

Marriage had certainly complicated life for Mr Pett, as it frequently does for the man who waits fifty years before trying it. P. G. WODEHOUSE

A man who forgets what day he was married, when he's been married one year, will forget, at about the end of the fourth, that he's married at all. P. G. WODEHOUSE

MEEKNESS
Wisdom has taught us to be calm and meek,
To take one blow, and turn the other cheek;
It is not written what a man shall do
If the rude caitiff smite the other too! O. W. HOLMES

It's going to be fun to see how long the meek can keep the earth when they inherit it. KIN HUBBARD

MEMORY
Forgetfulness is a gift from God bestowed upon debtors in compensation for their destitution of conscience.
AMBROSE BIERCE

It's a poor sort of memory that only works backwards.
LEWIS CARROLL

Women and elephants never forget. SAKI

A man's memory is what he forgets with. O. SHEPARD

MENTAL DEFICIENCY
He was the most backward boy in the form. He could not count beyond one and one, and even that sum he was liable to get wrong. BALAAM

It is more comfortable to be mad and not know it than to be sane and have one's doubts. G. B. BURGIN

"If you really were mad," said the young man, "you would think you must be sane. G. K. CHESTERTON

It's funny, the things you learn about lunatic asylums when you're actually in one. JONATHAN CLEMENTS

Great wits are sure to madness near allied.
JOHN DRYDEN (1631–1700)

The world often appears to be a lunatic asylum run by its inmates. LAMBERT JEFFRIES

MISFORTUNE
Calamities are of two kinds: misfortune to ourselves, and good fortune to others. AMBROSE BIERCE

"I'm a connoisseur of failure. I can smell it, roll it round my mouth, tell you the vintage." GILES COOPER

Nothing succeeds, they say, like success. And certainly nothing fails like failure. MARGARET DRABBLE

By trying, we can easily learn to endure adversity – another man's. MARK TWAIN

MODESTY
Modesty as a separate virtue scarcely exists. When it is sincere it is basically candour; when it is insincere it is hypocrisy. LAMBERT JEFFRIES

If one hides one's talent under a bushel one must be careful to point out to everyone the exact bushel under which it is hidden. SAKI

MONEY – *see also* ARISTOCRACY, BANKS, CLASS, FRIEND-SHIP, POVERTY.

That money talks
I'll not deny.
I heard it once –
It said "Good-bye".
RICHARD ARMOUR

Money speaks sense in a language all nations understand.
APHRA BEHN (1640–89)

Covet not aught, lest it should lead
You to commit some thieving deed.
Supply your wants a better way:
Buy what you want – and never pay. AMBROSE BIERCE

In time of war a sultan offered a camel-merchant paper money for his herd. The merchant returned to the sultan a sack of paper slips on each of which was written, "This is a camel". OSBERT BURDETT

To be clever enough to get all that money, one must be stupid enough to want it. G. K. CHESTERTON

"I have no money and therefore resolve to rail at all who have." WILLIAM CONGREVE (1670–1729)

A gift shop in Yorkshire has a sign which says: "Credit given only to customers over 85 – accompanied by both parents!" *Daily Telegraph*

Money nowadays seems to be produced with a natural homing instinct for the Treasury. DUKE OF EDINBURGH

It doesn't cost less because it's put on the account. A. G. ELLIOT

Most of the civil servants I know are immensely talented and charming young men, and it gives me a certain pleasure to think of them skilfully spending the money which I earned and which, left to myself, I should almost certainly have squandered. MICHAEL FRAYN

"You'd be surprised what people will put up with, if only they have to pay enough for it." RICHARD GORDON

"I should be a perfect dear
On fifty thousand pounds a year." A. P. HERBERT

That for which all virtue now is sold,
And almost every vice – almighty gold.
BEN JONSON (c. 1572–1637)

Grocers object to the forgery of cheques, which is a danger to their business, more than they object to the forgery of jam, which puts money in their purses. ROBERT LYND

Nice people, with nice habits, but they've got no money at all. NAT MILLS & FRED MALCOLM

When they're running short of money they borrow from each other. NAT MILLS & FRED MALCOLM

For one person who dreams of making fifty thousand pounds, a hundred people dream of being left fifty thousand pounds. A. A. MILNE

It's a waste of time trying to get your overdraft written off unless you are prepared to deprive yourself and family of such unnecessary luxuries as food, clothing, and shelter.
DENIS NORDEN

"What a lot of money! Do you mean to say the dinner cost all that?"
    "I've paid the bill. This is the tip." *Punch*

My father told me that if humanly possible one should never lend people money, as it almost inevitably made them hate you. LORD ROTHSCHILD

"I'm living so far beyond my income that we may almost be said to be living apart." SAKI

"When I meet a man who makes a hundred thousand a year, I take off my hat." GEORGE BERNARD SHAW

Poverty is no disgrace to a man, but it is confoundedly inconvenient. SYDNEY SMITH

A Rolls is the only possible car, especially when you're broke. You don't need to carry a penny in your pocket. Nobody dares to question your credit rating.
JACK THOMAS (quoting a con man)

I've been poor and I've been rich – rich is better.
SOPHIE TUCKER

Let us all live within our means, even if we have to borrow money to do it. ARTEMUS WARD

"I don't owe a penny to a single soul – not counting tradesmen. of course." P. G. WODEHOUSE

MOTORING – *see also* ACCIDENTS, CARS, RAILWAY, ROADS, TRAVEL.

It was but the work of a second for me to sense the danger. It was but the work of half a second, however, for us to be rustling our way... into the foliage of the bush.
ROBERT BENCHLEY

The nearest I came to death on the whole expedition [a two-man flight in a small aircraft] was in a car half an hour after we had put the aeroplane away. K. C. GANDAR DOWER

O woman in our hours of ease,
When empty roads invite and please,
Inciting us to cautious speed –
Then dost thou cry, "Take heed, take heed!"

When lorries loom on every side,
When roads are narrow and cars wide,
And driving is a constant worry –
Then dost thou cry, "Oh, hurry, hurry!" LAMBERT JEFFRIES

No wife should be permitted to travel in a car driven by her husband without a special licence... The behaviour of the ordinary wife in a husband-driven motor-car is a mere mockery of the garage-tie. E. V. KNOX

Second-hand car dealers, like cats, can sense when someone is afraid of them. DENIS NORDEN

His absent-mindedness made him a very dangerous, very slow driver, and since I was often seated next to him, he was known to change gears with my kneecap. PETER USTINOV

A Yorkshire farmer had been stopped by the police because only one of his rear lights was working. The police recorded his words as he walked round to the back of his vehicle: "To hell with the lights, where's the trailer?" JOHN WATSON

MURDER – *see also* CRIME, DEATH, PRISON.
"If the murderer is wise he will let well alone, but murderers are seldom wise." AGATHA CHRISTIE

Every murderer is probably somebody's old friend.
AGATHA CHRISTIE

If once a man indulges himself in murder, very soon he comes to think very little of robbing, and from robbing he comes next to drinking and Sabbath breaking, and from that to incivility and procrastination. Once begin upon this downward path, you never know where you are to stop.
THOMAS DE QUINCEY

We now sentence murderers to Life Imprisonment, which means they are let out after a few years. LAMBERT JEFFRIES

Almost everyone who has committed a murder knows that the business has its tragic side. ROBERT LYND

Baudelaire used to shock the citizens of Brussels by opening his conversation in cafés in a raised voice with the words: "The night I killed my father." ROBERT LYND

MUSIC

One ought to pack one's ears with cotton wool at a concert where Sir Henry Wood conducts. Otherwise the music is apt to distract one's attention. W. N. P. BARBELLION

Brass bands are all very well in their place – outside and several miles away. THOMAS BEECHAM

Singers have the most marvellous breath control and can kiss for at least ten minutes without stopping. JILLY COOPER

We had to play quietly because it was a very select place (Ciro's Club)... The members didn't want to be disturbed. BILLY COTTON

I bought a second-hand grand piano at Harrods, which contributed richness and joy to my room, and considerable pain to the lodgers above and below it. NOEL COWARD

The Irishman tried to prove his genius for music by explaining that his brother could play the German flute. GEORGE DARLEY

I'm a flute-player, not a flautist. I don't have a flaut and I've never flauted. JAMES GALWAY

The traditional exhibitionism on the first and last nights of the Prom season... has nothing to do with music but everything to do with the accident that it is all being televised. SPIKE HUGHES

The organ blew a thin Puritan-preacher's note through one of its hundred nostrils. ALDOUS HUXLEY

"Bad luck about young Jim. He wanted to be a pop star, but had to give up when they found out he could sing." LAMBERT JEFFRIES

Stravinsky's music used to be original. Now it is aboriginal.
ERNEST NEWMAN

My singing voice is to melody roughly what bubble-gum is to
gourmet cuisine. DENIS NORDEN

The general aim in music is to make other people... feel
outsiders, compared to yourself. STEPHEN POTTER

Thither came in shoals the intensely musical ... and in still
greater numbers the merely musical, who know how
Tchaikovsky's name is pronounced and can recognize several
of Chopin's nocturnes if you give them due warning. SAKI

A fine singer, after dinner, is to be avoided... One of the best
ways to put him down is to applaud him vociferously as soon
as he has sung the first verse, as if all was over.
W. M. THACKERAY

My friends tell me that my rendering of a Scarlatti sonata
sounds best from the garden. WYNFORD VAUGHAN-THOMAS

Tenors are noble, pure, and heroic, and get the soprano. But
baritones are born villains. LEONARD WARREN

It's very odd about George and music. You know, his parents
were quite normal. DUKE OF WINDSOR (of his nephew, Lord
Harewood, Director of English National Opera)

NAMES
The Ancient Mariner wouldn't have taken so well if it had
been called *The Old Sailor*. SAMUEL BUTLER

Suppose our word for rose had come from the Nether-
lands... anglicized as "stinkbloom". What follows? "My love
is like a red, red stinkbloom." ARTHUR MARSHALL

Groucho is not my real name. I'm breaking it in for a friend.
GROUCHO MARX

The common Welsh name Bzjxxllwcp is pronounced Jackson. MARK TWAIN

NECESSITY
Necessity makes an honest man a knave. DANIEL DEFOE

Necessity never made a good bargain. BENJAMIN FRANKLIN

Necessity is the smotherer of convention.
LAMBERT JEFFRIES

NEWSPAPERS – see also JOURNALISM.
The satisfied grunt of the *Daily Mail*, the abandoned gurgle of the *Sunday Times*, and the shrill enthusiastic scream of the *Daily Express*. (Dramatic critics) NOEL COWARD

"News is what a chap who doesn't care much about anything wants to read." EVELYN WAUGH

OBESITY – see also BODY.
Our wonderful Human Machine . . . is made up of countless billions of little cells called "cells", and it is the special duty of some of these little body cells to store up fat. And I will say this for them: they do their duty. ROBERT BENCHLEY

I'm so fat that when I have my shoes cleaned I have to take the shoeshine boy's word for it. STUBBY KAYE

She fitted into my largest armchair as if it had been built round her by somebody who knew they were wearing armchairs tight about the hips that season. P. G. WODEHOUSE

I'm so fat that when I take a shower my feet stay dry.
STUBBY KAYE

OIL
I never saw such a thing as paraffin oil is to ooze. We kept it in
the nose of the boat, and from there it oozed down to the
rudder, impregnating the whole boat... It oozed over the
river, and saturated the scenery. J. K. JEROME

OPINION – *see also* ADVICE, ARGUMENT, BIGOTRY.
When I want your opinion I'll give it to you.
LAURENCE PETER

Refusing to have an opinion is a way of having one.
LUIGI PIRANDELLO

When people agree with me I always feel I must be wrong.
OSCAR WILDE

PARENTS – *see also* BABIES, CHILDREN, RELATIONS.
Parents are the last people on earth who ought to have
children. SAMUEL BUTLER

He is too experienced a parent to make positive promises.
CHRISTOPHER MORLEY

Have you a young daughter about fifteen? Have a heart to heart talk with her on the facts of life. Believe me, you'll learn plenty. VIC OLIVER

I like the story about the Hampstead bookseller who put up a notice in his shop saying, "Children of Progressive Parents admitted only on leads". OLIVER PRITCHETT

Parents are the bones upon which children sharpen their teeth. PETER USTINOV

"To lose one parent may be regarded as a misfortune; to lose both looks like carelessness." OSCAR WILDE

The thing that impresses me most about America is the way parents obey their children. DUKE OF WINDSOR

PARTIES
I learnt to find my way about at parties, and can locate upstairs libraries and hideaways with rare cunning, so that I am practically never hooked in on games of chance.
ROBERT BENCHLEY

A drinks party... normally consists of a room packed full of people, all rapidly talking to each other while eagerly looking for someone else. CINDY BLAKE

On my eleventh birthday our house had been filled with friends, and the more enterprising of them had broken all the springs of the drawing-room sofa whilst using it as a trampoline. From then on my mother set her face against house-parties. R. F. DELDERFIELD

A Portsmouth party-goer was left chained naked to some

railings. When released, he fled wearing a borrowed grass skirt and two coconuts. Said a neighbour: "I thought it was disgusting. You expect this kind of behaviour at the weekend but not in the middle of the week." CHARLES NEVIN

I don't know how you feel about going to parties in fancy dress, but as a source of pleasure I have always ranked it somewhere on a level with cleaning the oven. DENIS NORDEN

Those who promote and organize the most riotous Christmas parties are seldom those who have one's best interests at heart. CHRISTOPHER WARD

PEOPLE
Sidney and Beatrice Webb – two nice people if ever there was one. ALAN BENNETT

Lovers of Humanity generally hate people and children.
ROY CAMPBELL

Every man has one thing he can do better than anyone else, and usually it is reading his own handwriting.
NORMAN COLLIE

"He's been trained as a gentleman's gentleman – they're always much more reliable than gentlemen." NOEL COWARD

"Never trust men with short legs – brains too near their bottoms!" NOEL COWARD

"I know he is a truly great and good man, for he told me so himself." W. S. GILBERT

PESSIMISM – see also CYNICISM, FRUSTRATION.
The optimist proclaims that we live in the best of all possible worlds; the pessimist fears that this is true.
JAMES BRANCH CABELL

Nothing to do but work,
  Nothing to eat but food,
Nothing to wear but clothes,
  To keep one from going nude. BEN KING

A pessimist is a man who looks both ways before crossing a one-way street. LAURENCE J. PETER

A pessimist is one who, when he has the choice of two evils, chooses both. OSCAR WILDE

PHILOSOPHY – *see also* THOUGHTS.
Philosophy: unintelligible answers to insoluble problems. HENRY ADAMS

Voltaire is reported to have said: *Plus ça change, plus ça reste* – meaning, "There isn't much sense doing anything these days". ROBERT BENCHLEY

Philosophers are adults who persist in asking childish questions. ISAIAH BERLIN

Philosophy: a route of many roads leading from nowhere to nothing. AMBROSE BIERCE

Scientific thought is saying in hard words and involved sentences what could better be said in easy ones.
SAMUEL BUTLER

An open mind is all very well in its way, but it ought not to be so open that there is no keeping anything in or out of it.
SAMUEL BUTLER

Don't state the matter plainly,
  But put it in a hint;
Learn to look at all things
  With a sort of mental squint. LEWIS CARROLL

He that thinks himself the happiest man really is so, but he that thinks himself the wisest is generally the greatest fool.
C. C. COLTON

"I long ago came to the conclusion that nothing has ever been definitely proved about anything." NOEL COWARD

Philosophers have always been happier in felling the orchards of their predecessors than in planting new ones.
LAMBERT JEFFRIES

Rousseau fixed the summit of his earthly bliss at living in an orchard with an amiable woman and a cow, and he never attained even that. He did get as far as the orchard, but the woman was not amiable, and she brought her mother with her, and there was no cow. J. K. JEROME

"Dying for an idea" sounds well enough, but why not let the idea die instead of you? P. WYNDHAM LEWIS

Give us the luxuries of life and we will dispense with the necessaries. J. L. MOTLEY

If anything *can* go wrong, it will. *Murphy's Law*

A mouse never trusts its life to a single hole. PLAUTUS

For there was never yet philosopher
That could endure the toothache patiently.
WILLIAM SHAKESPEARE *(Much Ado About Nothing)*

Philosophers have scattered through the world as many plagues of the mind as Pandora's box did those of the body.
JONATHAN SWIFT (1667–1745)

Being a philosopher, I have a problem for every solution.
ROBERT ZEND

PLACES – *see also* **FRANCE, WALES.**
Earth is here (Australia) so kind that just tickle her with a hoe and she laughs with a harvest. DOUGLAS JERROLD

Oudna (N. Africa) was a must for suicides, a barren plain bisected by a Roman Aqueduct ... We arrived in a great cloud of dust which improved the place. SPIKE MILLIGAN

Most of the geography of Scotland consists of mountains, grass, heather, and Edinburgh. FRANK MUIR

His mother lived at Bethnal Green, which was not altogether his fault. SAKI

PLATITUDE
Platitude: a thought that snores. AMBROSE BIERCE

Even a platitude dropped from a sufficiently great height can sound like a brick. PEREGRINE WORSTHORNE

PLATONIC LOVE
Platonic love is love from the neck up. THYRA S. WINSLOW

PLEASURE
Business was his aversion; pleasure was his business.
MARIA EDGEWORTH

POETRY – *see also* **BOOKS, LIBRARIES, PROSE, QUOTATIONS, WRITING.**
A poet can earn much more money writing or talking about his art than he can by practising it. W. H. AUDEN

For a man to be a poet ... he must be in love, or miserable.
LORD BYRON

Poetry is not a career but a mug's game. T. S. ELIOT

It's hard to say why writing verse
Should terminate in drink, or worse. A. P. HERBERT

I never knowed a successful man who could quote poetry.
KIN HUBBARD

Dr Donne's poems are like the peace of God: they pass all
understanding. KING JAMES I (1566–1625)

Perhaps no person can be a poet, or can even enjoy poetry,
without a certain unsoundness of mind. T. B. MACAULAY

POLITENESS – *see also* **ETIQUETTE.**
"Old Evans ... holds the door open for his wife just because
we're there. We know damn well he goes back to slamming it
in her face the minute we've gone home." ALAN AYCKBOURN

They say courtesy costs nothing, but it's surprising how many
people can't seem to afford it. J. BASIL BOOTHROYD

"You must admit he's always courteous to his inferiors."
"Where does he find them?" DOROTHY PARKER

I beg your pardon for calling on you in this informal way, but
your house is on fire. MARK TWAIN (to new neighbour)

A gentleman is a man who gets up to open the door for his
wife to bring the coal in. ANON

POLITICS
All kinds of accents are heard in the House of Commons. A
Member of Parliament is no more required to pass a test in
standard speech than he is required to take an intelligence
test. BALAAM

I met Curzon... from whom I got the sort of greeting a corpse would give to an undertaker. STANLEY BALDWIN (Lord Curzon had hoped to be Prime Minister instead of Baldwin.)

The whole art of political speech is to put *nothing* into it. It is much more difficult than it sounds. HILAIRE BELLOC

I don't go to the House of Lords any more. I went once but my umbrella was stolen by a bishop. LORD BERNERS

All I can feel about leadership struggle is let them struggle, and let's just pray that when someone's come out on top we shan't get an instant paperback by a couple of political journalists telling us how it all happened.
J. BASIL BOOTHROYD

"Those who would enjoy the pleasures of democracy," said the Doctor, "must school themselves to suffer the law's delay." IVOR BROWN

Wives (of politicians) never know whether they're snoozing on the back bench, chairing a committee meeting, or carrying on an affaire of state. JILLY COOPER

"All this session the Government's supporters have been literally glued to the benches." *Daily Telegraph* (quoting)

As a politician never believes what he says, he is surprised when others believe him. CHARLES DE GAULLE

The ministers on the Treasury Bench remind me of a marine landscape on the coast of South America. You behold a range of exhausted volcanoes. BENJAMIN DISRAELI

But then the prospect of a lot
  Of dull M.P.'s in close proximity,
All thinking for themselves, is what
  No man can face with equanimity. W. S. GILBERT

There are too many men in politics – and not enough elsewhere. HERMIONE GINGOLD

Treason doth never prosper. What's the reason?
If it doth prosper, none dare call it treason.
JOHN HARINGTON (1611–1677)

The Commons must bray like an ass every day
  To appease their electoral hordes. A. P. HERBERT

If only the House of Commons had emulated the Lords' admirable inactivity, we should have been saved from a great many foolish Acts. LAMBERT JEFFRIES

I must follow them: I am their leader.
A. BONAR LAW (attributed)

Although he provided the opinions himself, he always depended upon his secretary for the arguments with which to support them. A. A. MILNE

For years politicians have promised people the moon. I'm the first one able to deliver it. RICHARD NIXON (message to astronauts)

It's as dark as the mind of a politician. MORLEY ROBERTS

We all know that Prime Ministers are wedded to the truth, but like other married couples they sometimes live apart. SAKI

Mr Gladstone said he was trying to learn to sleep in the House of Commons. KATE STANLEY

The leaders of our two main parties are to each other exactly as are the two champions of the boxing ring who knock each other about for the belt and £500. ANTHONY TROLLOPE

POVERTY – *see also* MONEY.
People don't resent having nothing nearly as much as having too little. IVY COMPTON-BURNETT

There may be a pleasure in poverty, but it is a retrospective one. LAMBERT JEFFRIES

Being poor is a mere trifle. It is being known to be poor that is the sting. J. K. JEROME

"Have you ever known what it's like to be without in the midst of plenty?"
  "Indeed I have. Wasn't I once caretaker in a girls' school?" DENIS NORDEN

The less money you have, the less you worry. GEORGE ORWELL

The truly poor man is not he who has little but he who wishes for more. SENECA

Very few people can afford to be poor.
GEORGE BERNARD SHAW

My mother's idea of economy was to take a bus to the Ritz.
LADY TRUMPINGTON

PRACTICAL JOKING
Adrian had a fit of insomnia, and amused himself by
unscrewing and transposing all the bedroom numbers. SAKI

PRISON – *see also* CRIME, MURDER, STEALING.
The only thing I really mind about going to prison is the
thought of Lord Longford coming to visit me.
RICHARD INGRAMS

Prison: a guest house with so many amenities that many of its
patrons are quite happy to return. LAMBERT JEFFRIES

Anyone who has been to an English public school will always
feel comparatively at home in prison. EVELYN WAUGH

PROGRESS
What we call progress is the exchange of one nuisance for
another nuisance. HAVELOCK ELLIS

Progress means deterioration.
PATRICK HUTBER (Hutber's Law)

The unreasonable man persists in trying to adapt the world to
himself. Therefore all progress depends on the unreasonable
man. GEORGE BERNARD SHAW

Is it progress if a cannibal uses a knife and fork?
STANISLAW LEC

PROPHECY – *see also* FORTUNE-TELLING.
Matrons who toss the cup, and see
The grounds of fate in grounds of tea.
CHARLES CHURCHILL

Prophecy is the most gratuitous form of error.
GEORGE ELIOT

You can only predict things after they've taken place.
EUGENE IONESCO

Prophets were stoned first in anger; then, after death, with
a handsome slab in the graveyard. CHRISTOPHER MORLEY

The wisest prophets make sure of the event first.
HORACE WALPOLE

PROSE – *see also* BOOKS, POETRY, WRITING.
I'm not very well today. I can only write prose.
W. B. YEATS (attributed)

PSYCHOLOGY
There is something wrong with a society in which parents are afraid to speak to their children without first consulting a psychologist. BALAAM

Anyone who goes to a psychiatrist ought to have his head examined. SAM GOLDWYN

Many who go into the profession (psychoanalysis) do so in order to overcome their own neurosis.
PROFESSOR ERNEST JONES

Because Professor Feynman answered an Army psychiatrist's questions truthfully he was thought to be insane.
STUART SUTHERLAND

QUOTATIONS – *see also* BOOKS, POETRY, WRITING.
Padding with quotes is usually done when the author is afraid to present his own opinion or else is anxious to show that he is widely read. PHILIP BONEWITS

Shake was a dramatist of note;
He lived by writing things to quote. H. C. BUNNER

It is a good thing for an uneducated man to read books of quotations. WINSTON CHURCHILL

We pay much more attention to a wise passage when it is quoted than when we read it in the original author.
P. G. HAMERTON

The Oxford Dictionary of Quotations quotes nearly all Shakespeare and Milton and Wordsworth, and so much of the Bible that if it wasn't published by the Oxford University Press there would be an infringement of copyright. E. V. KNOX

A quotation is a handy thing to have about, saving one the trouble of thinking for oneself. A. A. MILNE

The quotation of two or three lines from Spencer's *Faerie Queene* is probably as good a silencer as any.
STEPHEN POTTER

When in doubt, ascribe all quotations to Bernard Shaw.
NIGEL REES

I often quote myself: it adds spice to the conversation.
GEORGE BERNARD SHAW

RACING – *see also* CRICKET, GAMBLING, GAMES, HORSE, SPORT, TENNIS.
Lord Hippo suffered fearful loss
By putting money on a horse
Which he believed, if it were pressed,
Would run far faster than the rest. HILAIRE BELLOC

Everyone knows that racing is carried on chiefly for the delight and profit of fools, ruffians, and thieves.
GEORGE GISSING

Alas! it is the painful fact
That horses hardly ever act
As anyone expected. A. P. HERBERT

"I backed the right horse, but the wrong one went and won."
HENRY ARTHUR JONES & HENRY HERMAN

RAILWAY – *see also* CARS, MOTORING, ROADS, TRAVEL.
Probably the most common of all antagonisms arises from a man taking a seat beside you on a train. ROBERT BENCHLEY

I pick the loser every time. If ever you see me in a queue at the railway booking-office, join the other one; because there'll be a chap at the front of mine who's trying to send a rhinoceros to Tokyo. J. BASIL BOOTHROYD

To our dismay a rare thing happened – our train was punctual. JAN & CORA GORDON

O thou, the foe of comfort, heat,
O thou, who hast the corner seat...
Keeping the window down
Though all the carriage frown,
Why dost thou so rejoice in air? E. V. LUCAS

On Sunday I took a train, which didn't seem to want to go there, to Newcastle. J. B. PRIESTLEY

For safety in a train take a centre carriage and the right-hand seat; in case of a coming collision throw yourself either into the rack or under the seat. *Strand Magazine* (1911)

RELATIONS – *see also* ANCESTORS, PARENTS.
"Henceforth," said she sadly, "let us be to one another as brother and sister." "No," said I, as I thought of my own sisters, "not as bad as that." SAMUEL BUTLER

Father, Mother, and Me,
Sister and Auntie say
All the people like us are We,
And everyone else is They. RUDYARD KIPLING

A poor relation – is the most irrelevant thing in nature.
CHARLES LAMB

RELIGION – *see also* CHRISTMAS, CHURCH, HEAVEN,
SUPERSTITION.
He was of the faith chiefly in the sense that the church he
currently did not attend was Catholic. KINGSLEY AMIS

"It's a bit depressing if most of the congregation are in the
churchyard instead of the church." ALAN AYCKBOURN

"Gracious Lord, oh bomb the Germans.
  Spare the women for Thy Sake;
And if that is not too easy
  We will pardon Thy Mistake.
But gracious Lord, whate'er shall be,
Don't let anyone bomb me." JOHN BETJEMAN

The Bible is like the poor: we have it always with us but we
know very little about it. SAMUEL BUTLER

Ordination was something which he supposed would have to
be undergone some day but about which, as about dying,
there was no need to trouble himself yet. SAMUEL BUTLER

Tennyson has said that more things are wrought by prayer
than this world dreams of, but he has wisely refrained from
saying whether they are good things or bad things.
SAMUEL BUTLER

Religion is by no means a proper subject of conversation in a
mixed company. EARL OF CHESTERFIELD (1694–1773)

The Lent newsletter for St John's Church, Fareham, lists "Jesus speaks to the guilty – the Vicar".
Daily Telegraph

There are not many people who would care to sleep in a church. I don't mean at sermon-time... but at night and alone. CHARLES DICKENS

"Sensible men are all of the same religion."
"What is that?"
"Sensible men never tell." BENJAMIN DISRAELI

I dared to ask my History master, Tuppy Headlam, for his views on a future life. He replied, "Doubtless I shall inherit eternal bliss, but I prefer not to discuss so depressing a topic."
CHRISTOPHER HOLLIS

"At the present time the Anglican clergy wear their collars the wrong way round. I would compel them to wear, not only their collars, but all their clothes back to front."
ALDOUS HUXLEY

Half the rules seemed to forbid things he had never heard of;

and the other half forbade things he was doing every day and could not imagine not doing. C. S. LEWIS

Musical comedy songs have always tended to spread a little more happiness than the average hymn. ARTHUR MARSHALL

A little girl had just been assured that God could do anything. "Then, if he can do anything, can he make a stone so heavy that He can't lift it?" A. A. MILNE

We can't for a certainty tell
    What mirth may molest us on Monday;
But at least, to begin the week well,
    Let us all be unhappy on Sunday. CHARLES NEAVES

"No one can be an unbeliever nowadays. The Christian Apologists have left nothing to disbelieve." SAKI

God is a sort of burglar. As a young man you knock him down. As an old man you try to conciliate him for fear he may knock *you* down. H. BEERBOHM TREE

O Lord, thou knowest I have nine houses in the City of London and have lately purchased an estate in Essex. I beseech thee to preserve the counties of Middlesex and Essex from fires and earthquakes. JOSHUA WARD (d. 1761)

The other day I saw an advertisement for some job in the Church which specified that a knowledge of the Christian religion would be helpful. MICHAEL WHARTON

The Ten Commandments don't tell you what you ought to do, and only put ideas into your head. ANON

RESOLUTIONS
As soon as we make a good resolution we get into a situation which makes its observance unbearable. WILLIAM FEATHER

There is much to be said for putting a good resolution into effect now and then... If you make a resolve to get up at seven o'clock every day during the year, you should do it on at least one morning. ROBERT LYND

REVOLUTION
Everyone knows revolutions are – after football – the favourite occupation of the South Americans.
JACQUIE DURRELL

"There won't be any revolution in America... The people are too clean." ERIC LINKLATER

ROADS – *see also* CARS, MOTORING, RAILWAY, TRAVEL.
The rolling English drunkard made the rolling English road.
G. K. CHESTERTON

The noblest prospect which a Scotsman ever sees is the high road that leads him to England. SAMUEL JOHNSON

As soon as a road is covered with new asphalt, but before it dries, it is to be torn up again by the Gas authorities; the same procedure is to be repeated by the Water Board authorities; by the telephone linesmen; by the Sanitary authorities; by the Inland Revenue... GEORGE MIKES

SCHOOL – *see also* CHILDREN, EDUCATION, TEACHERS, UNIVERSITY.
The headmaster held very strongly that children are best left to teach themselves... This comfortable doctrine not only saved him a deal of labour, the purchase of books, and the maintenance of ushers, but exercised a profound impression on the minds of progressive parents. IVOR BROWN

"That's the reason they're called lessons," the Gryphon remarked; "because they lessen from day to day."
LEWIS CARROLL

To my father a school was not a seat of learning but a noisy detention compound to which children were sent for long periods of the year in order to be removed from under their parents' feet. R. F. DELDERFIELD

I used to visit the lavatories when I was frightened, and as I was frightened most of the time I got to know the lavatories pretty well. LUDOVIC KENNEDY

My daughter once... padlocked herself to the front door with a bicycle chain and maintained that she had swallowed the key, saying, "Now perhaps you'll believe me when I tell you I hate school." ROBERT MORLEY

You can't expect a boy to be depraved until he has been to a good school. SAKI

I liked Eton, except in the following respects: for work and games, for boys and masters. OSBERT SITWELL

I went to Winchester in 1840 at twelve years old, able to work a quadratic equation well, and left it at eighteen, competent to perform the same task badly. W. TUCKWELL

SCIENCE
The real joy of science is escaping from all the ordinary pressures of existence into a world where you can be completely happy doing something quite absorbing and largely useless. J. BASIL BOOTHROYD

"You see (said Alice) the earth takes twenty-four hours to turn round on its axis." "Talking of axes," said the Duchess, "chop off her head!" LEWIS CARROLL

Miss Matty told me that she never could believe that the earth was moving constantly, and that she would not believe it if she could, it made her feel so tired and dizzy whenever she thought about it. E. C. GASKELL

Science, which can do so much, cannot decide what it ought to do. J. W. KRUTCH

If an experiment works, something has gone wrong.
Murphy's Law

SEASICKNESS – *see also* **BOATS.**
How holy people look when they are seasick!
SAMUEL BUTLER

It is a curious fact, but nobody is ever seasick on land.
J. K. JEROME

Wilfred Grenfell was seasick most of the passage... Characteristically he fought the weakness by going into the open and running backwards and forwards as best he could on the tilting and lifting deck. J. LENNOX KERR

I am enchanted with my own company, but not when I'm being seasick. LORD MANCROFT

April 7. The wind grew high. I began to be dizzy and squeamish. My Lord sent for me to come down and eat some oysters... All the afternoon I walked upon the deck to keep myself from being sick. SAMUEL PEPYS (1633–1703)

If there is one thing in the world to make a man insufferably conceited, it is to have his stomach behave itself when nearly all his comrades are seasick. MARK TWAIN

SEASIDE– *see also* **BOATS, HOLIDAYS.**
Sand in the sandwiches, wasps in the tea,
Sun on our bathing-dresses, heavy with the wet...
Fleas in the tamarisk, an early cigarette. JOHN BETJEMAN

How cold the bathe, how chattering cold the drying!
JOHN BETJEMAN

There's sand in the porridge and sand in the bed,
And if this is pleasure we'd sooner be dead! NOEL COWARD

I do like to be beside the seaside! JOHN GLOVER-KIND

"My wife and I took this commodious residence for six weeks
and engaged the sea at great expense to come up to our doors
twice a day." A. A. MILNE

Some people wore summer clothes in a hopeful, goose-
pimpled way. PAUL THEROUX

SELFISHNESS – *see also* **EGOTISM.**
The idea of minding our own business is rubbish. Who could
be so selfish? MYRTLE BARKER

Unselfishness is what we do for others. Selfishness is what
they fail to do for us. LAMBERT JEFFRIES

Self-love is not so vile a sin
As self-neglect. WILLIAM SHAKESPEARE *(Henry V)*

SEX – *see also* **CHASTITY, KISSING, LOVE, MARRIAGE.**
"I enjoy it for what it's worth and fully intend to go on doing
so for as long as anybody is interested, and when the time
comes that they're not I shall be perfectly content to settle
down with an apple and a good book." NOEL COWARD

My husband believes that a Casanova provides a useful social service, claiming that the best women, like Rolls-Royces, should be delivered to the customer fully run in.
JILLY COOPER

Men's pupils dilate more at the sight of a female pin-up than vice versa. JOHN FISHER

The difference between sex for money and sex for free is that sex for money usually costs a lot less. BRENDAN FRANCIS

A bird in the bed is worth two in the bushes.
LAMBERT JEFFRIES

Her dachshund, she said, was oversexed. Could I please do something to damp his ardour. Well, indeed I could. I recommended the remedy that has damped male ardour since time began. I found him a wife. BUSTER LLOYD-JONES

Whoever named it necking was a poor judge of anatomy.
GROUCHO MARX

Contraceptives should be used on every conceivable occasion.
SPIKE MILLIGAN

Men rarely make passes
At girls wearing glasses. DOROTHY PARKER

Come up and see me sometime.
MAE WEST (supposed saying)

Any time you got nothin' to do and lots of time to do it, come
on up. MAE WEST (actual saying)

My life is an open book. All too often open at the wrong page.
MAE WEST

If I asked for a cup of coffee, someone would search for the
double meaning. MAE WEST

When I'm good I'm very very good, but when I'm bad, I'm
better. MAE WEST

Give a man a free hand and he'll try and put it all over you
MAE WEST

SHAKESPEARE – *see also* THEATRE.
I don't think I should want to know Shakespeare. I know him
as well as I want by knowing his plays. JONATHAN MILLER

It does not follow... that the right to criticize Shakespeare
involves the power of writing better plays.
GEORGE BERNARD SHAW

He had read Shakespeare and found him weak in chemistry.
H. G. WELLS

SHOPPING
If you want to buy something in a junk shop, ask for
something else... It causes the enemy to concentrate on the
wrong flank. JOYCE CARY

They say the supermarket has simplified life. I don't know. For a start, if you get in the wrong traffic lane, you can be shoved round the place backwards by a tide of implacable housewives. J. BASIL BOOTHROYD

Confectioners caught on that customers would happily buy a hole if it had a bit of mint round it. FRANK MUIR

SLEEP – *see also* **BED, DREAMS.**
The great artist in sleep is the domestic cat. Who has ever seen a cat attempting to sleep by sitting bolt upright in a train, then allowing itself to sag to one side, roll its eyes upwards, and open its mouth till its teeth nearly fall out. HYLTON CLEAVER

A reader collecting sleeping pills from the local chemist found written on the bottle: "One to be taken at night. Warning – this may cause drowsiness." *Daily Telegraph*

I don't know why it should be, I am sure, but the sight of another man asleep in bed when I am up, maddens me.
J. K. JEROME

No cure for snoring? We had a most reliable one at Sherborne forty-five years ago – dropping specially kept pellets of soap into the offending mouth. LETTER IN *The Times*

SMOKING

There is nothing [in a hotel] to stop you from smoking a pipe full of damp shredded socks and blowing the smoke all round the dining-room. CLEMENT FREUD

I have smoked "carefully blended" mixtures that tasted like a hayrick on fire. J. B. PRIESTLEY

Nicotine is an awful curse,
It strains the heart and drains the purse. K. T. SARMA

I have made it a rule never to smoke more than one cigar at a time. MARK TWAIN

SMUGNESS – *see also* EGOTISM.

I wish I was as cocksure of anything as Tom Macaulay is of everything. VISCOUNT MELBOURNE

SNOWSHOES

Snowshoes are like horses. They know when they are carrying a novice and do as they please, choosing their own direction. F. D. OMMANNEY

SOLITUDE

Alone: in bad company. AMBROSE BIERCE

There is something rather stimulating and exciting about being in an empty place where there is no life but one's own. ALDOUS HUXLEY

Never less alone than when alone. SAMUEL ROGERS

Girls who wear zippers shouldn't live alone. J. VAN DRUTEN

People could with advantage be compelled to remain absolutely alone for several hours a day. P. WYNDHAM LEWIS

SPACE

Nothing puzzles me more than time and space, and yet nothing puzzles me less, for I never think about them.
CHARLES LAMB

I have never really understood what we hope to gain by sending eight people whizzing round the world ... for ninety days at a cost of 35 thousand dollars per hour per person.
AUBERON WAUGH

SPEECH

The Liza Doolittle who exclaims, "He's off his chump, he is, I don't want no balmies teaching me" is better worth listening to than the Miss Doolittle who intones with laboured precision: "So pleased to *have* met you." BALAAM

What he said was excellent, but there can be too much of an excellent thing. HENRY CECIL

[After a brief stay in Paris] our vocabularies were the richer by several French phrases, and three complete sentences, two of which were unrepeatable. NOEL COWARD

With foreigners I find my voice rising and my ideas fading away. M. DONALDSON-HUDSON

That vixen tongue of yours, my dear,
Alarms our neighbours far and near:
Good God! 'tis like a rolling river
That murm'ring flows, and flows for ever.
JOHN GAY (1685–1732)

The dog, considered a sagacious beast,
Does not give tongue when he has had a feast.
Nor does the cow go mooing round the mead
To tell the world that she's enjoyed her feed ...
But Modern Man, by some malignant fate,

When he has eaten, simply must orate. A. P. HERBERT

And when you stick on conversation's burrs,
Don't strew your pathway with those dreadful "-ers".
O. W. HOLMES

His voice, when he spoke and especially when he raised it in preaching, was harsh, like the grating of iron hinges when a seldom-used door is opened. ALDOUS HUXLEY

It is a fantasy that if you got lots of interesting and famous people together you would have the best conversation possible. You wouldn't at all. You'd have envy, competition, rancour, and the whole thing would be very boring.
JONATHAN MILLER

Val chattered away happily every moment of her waking day. She never said anything; just talked. FRANK MUIR

It is remarkable that they
Talk most who have the least to say. MATTHEW PRIOR

She spoke with the breathless haste of one to whom repartee comes as rarely as the finding of a gold-handled umbrella.
SAKI

It was her invariable plan to speak in a sleepy, comfortable voice whenever she was unusually keen about anything; it put people off their guard. SAKI

Today's witty conversationalist is tomorrow's bore.
ANNE SCOTT-JAMES

"I don't want to talk grammar. I want to talk like a lady."
GEORGE BERNARD SHAW

"When I say an ill-natured thing 'tis out of pure good-humour." R. B. SHERIDAN

He has occasional flashes of silence that make his conversation perfectly delightful.
SYDNEY SMITH (of Macaulay)

He deserves to be preached to death by wild curates.
SYDNEY SMITH

Ida never spoke, she just said what she pleased.
GERTRUDE STEIN

That's as well said as if I had said it myself.
JONATHAN SWIFT (1667–1745)

I have often regretted my speech, never my silence.
PUBLILIUS SYRUS

His answers were so final and exact that he did not leave a doubt to hang conversation on. MARK TWAIN

SPORT – *see also* CRICKET, EXERCISE, GAMES, TENNIS.
Good losers get into the habit of losing. GEORGE ALLEN

The school Sports Day is a purgatory of tedium ... Exciting finishes are rare oases in a desert of dullness, and always happen when I am looking at something else. BALAAM

I used to do a bit of boxing. They called me "Washing" because I was always hanging on the ropes. LES DAWSON

One shouts "Boomerang!" People unaware of which direction the thing is coming from... flex their knees just a little, hunch their shoulders just a little, and begin to raise their hands as if to protect their ears. ALAN COREN

Members of the Berkshire Golf Club believe that the game of golf should be played briskly. "If God had meant a round to take more than three hours, he would never have invented Sunday lunch," they argue. JIMMY HILL

The green is, in the golf religion, the counterpart of the sanctuary, which surrounds the cup or hole which is, in golf, the sacrosanct equivalent of the altar. JOHN MARSHALL

Serious sport has nothing to do with fair play... It is war minus the shooting. GEORGE ORWELL

If all the year were playing holidays,
To sport would be as tedious as to work.
WILLIAM SHAKESPEARE *(Henry IV, Pt I)*

The people who control sport in this country carry on as if it never rained. MICHAEL WALE

I play no outdoor games, except dominoes. I have sometimes played dominoes outside French cafés. OSCAR WILDE

STEALING – *see also* CRIME, PRISON.
Don't steal; thou'lt never thus compete
Successfully in business. Cheat. AMBROSE BIERCE

Ambidextrous: able to pick a pocket with either hand.
AMBROSE BIERCE

A burglar who respects his art always takes his time before he takes anything else. O. HENRY

A store detective said he'd seen a lot of people who were so confused that they'd stolen things, but never any so confused that they'd paid twice. BARONESS PHILLIPS

STUPIDITY – *see also* IGNORANCE.
There's a sucker born ever minute. P. T. BARNUM

Idiot: a member of a large and powerful tribe whose influence on human affairs has always been dominant.
AMBROSE BIERCE

A fool must now and then be right by chance.
WILLIAM COWPER

"I simply can't bear fools." "Apparently your mother did not have the same difficulty." DOROTHY PARKER

SUCCESS
The toughest thing about success is that you've got to keep on being a success. IRVING BERLIN

Success is the one unpardonable sin against one's fellows.
AMBROSE BIERCE

He was a self-made man who owed his lack of success to nobody. JOSEPH HELLER

Failures are the steps that lead to success. Success is the blind alley at the top of the steps. LAMBERT JEFFRIES

For one person spoilt by success, a thousand are spoilt by failure. LAMBERT JEFFRIES

Success makes people, for the most part, humble, tolerant, and kind. Failure makes people bitter and cruel.
W. SOMERSET MAUGHAM

Nothing recedes like success. WALTER WINCHELL

SUPERCILIOUSNESS

He would say, "You want a wash, I expect," in a way which suggested he had spotted two dirty finger-nails.
STEPHEN POTTER

SUPERSTITION

Superstition is the religion of feeble minds. EDMUND BURKE

"I never gets sea boils," an old chap told me. "That's because I always cuts my nails on a Monday." WILFRED GRENFELL

Faith is what we believe in but cannot prove. Superstitition is what other people believe in but cannot prove.
LAMBERT JEFFRIES

Loch Ness has not got a monster in it, but the locals are keeping the fact quiet. FRANK MUIR

As soon as civilizations grow out of one set of superstitions they replace them with a new lot. FRANK MUIR

Most primitive people are very careful to destroy all their nail-cuttings and hair-clippings, since they believe that a witch might use these to work them harm. H. S. REDGROVE

TEACHERS – *see also* EDUCATION, SCHOOL, UNIVERSITY.

I can remember few of the teachers, because they were there so briefly, for a term or less. Most had the furtive air of being on the run. KENNETH ALLSOP

A teacher tells me he once saw the following comment written by a colleague on a pupil's school report: "His spelling is absolutly apalling". BALAAM

The dangerous practice of striking a boy with the hand the headmaster could not approve, so he burst out with the immortal words: "If any boy talks, give him a good hard *push!*" BALAAM

My first headmaster was a headmistress, and I can remember her quite clearly, although I was only a mixed infant at the time. J. BASIL BOOTHROYD

A Harrow master... made the boys in his House football team eat the stodgiest possible pudding before a match – either from a dislike of football or from a dislike of boys. G. F. LAMB

Every schoolmaster knows that for every one person who wants to teach there are approximately thirty who don't want to learn. W. C. SELLAR & R. J. YEATMAN

"I have been long enough in the teaching profession to know that no one enters it unless he has some very good reason that he is anxious to conceal." EVELYN WAUGH

Assistant masters came and went... Some liked little boys too little and some too much. EVELYN WAUGH

After a year's training, if the student showed little sign of coping with a class, and if I felt the case was hopeless, I would advise him to become an assistant in a local public library. In the course of the years I made quite a number of librarians. J. DOVER WILSON

TELEPHONE
Telephone: an invention of the devil which abrogates some of the advantages of making a disagreeable person keep his distance. AMBROSE BIERCE

If you particularly want to be left alone to brood over your problems, the telephone is sure to ring. P. G. WODEHOUSE

TELEVISION AND RADIO – *see also* CINEMA, THEATRE.
Television is chewing-gum for the eyes.
FRED ALLEN (attributed)

Television is something you appear on: you don't watch it.
NOEL COWARD

A card in a Portsmouth shop window read: "For sale. Grey
African parrot, profuse talker, filthy language. Would suit
TV playwright." *Daily Telegraph*

I'll believe in colour television when I see it in black and
white. SAM GOLDWYN

The main and most glorious achievement of television is that
it is killing the art of conversation. If we think of the type of
conversation television is helping to kill, our gratitude must
be undying. GEORGE MIKES

It was one of those very serious investigative programmes in
which young interviewers in dreadful little overcoats stopped
people in the streets and asked them things. FRANK MUIR

He was a shortish, middle-aged man with a look of uneasy
jauntiness, like those minor relatives who swarm on at the
end of *This Is Your Life*. DENIS NORDEN

Television is entertainment that flows like tap-water.
DENNIS POTTER

These days a star is anyone who can hold a microphone.
HARRY SECOMBE

Either Oxford or Cambridge is leading.
JOHN SNAGGE (commentary on the Boat Race)

Usually my video recorder records programmes I don't want
to see, and then plays them back when I'm out. ERNIE WISE

I'm not in love with Television. I'm easily embarrassed, and I don't like loads of people around me when I'm showing off. TERRY WOGAN

Some of those old film epics you can see with monotonous regularity cost less to make than many of the brief TV commercials that come in between them! ANON

One of the unarguable facts of life is that you get noticed a lot more on TV than you do in any other media. ANON

TEMPTATION
"You ought not to yield to temptation." "Well, somebody must or the thing becomes absurd." ANTHONY HOPE

"I never resist temptation because I have found that the things that are bad for me never tempt me.' GEORGE BERNARD SHAW

I generally avoid temptation, unless I can't resist it. MAE WEST

The only way to get rid of temptation is to yield to it. OSCAR WILDE

I can resist anything except temptation. OSCAR WILDE

TENNIS – *see also* CRICKET, GAMES, RACING, SPORT.
I've been told that one of these modern players was so busy bouncing the ball that he quite forgot to serve. LAMBERT JEFFRIES

Some players look at linesmen more in sorrow than in anger, but others, like McEnroe, are more like spoilt children screaming to get their own way. LAMBERT JEFFRIES

As an irascible veteran, Gardnar Mulloy once removed his glasses and offered them to an erring linesman.
PAUL METZLER

"What about apologizing?" my partner went on. 'Shall we do it after every stroke, or at the end of each game, or when we say good-bye, or never? I get so tired of saying 'Sorry'."
A. A. MILNE

In the right hand court I use the American service, which means that I never know till the last moment which side of the racket is going to hit the ball. A. A. MILNE

To the Tennis Court, and there saw the King play; but to see how his play is extolled without any cause at all is a loathsome sight. SAMUEL PEPYS (1633–1703)

THEATRE – *see also* **CINEMA, CRITICISM, SHAKESPEARE, TELEVISION AND RADIO,**
A common weakness is to over-multiply the mysteries... Too many crooks spoil the broth. IVOR BROWN

Our poets make us laugh at Tragedy,
And with their Comedies they make us cry.
DUKE OF BUCKINGHAM (1628–1687)

The audience was tremendously fashionable, and, for the first part of the play *(Bittersweet)*, almost as responsive as so many cornflour blancmanges. NOEL COWARD

The orchestra, frantic with indecision as to whether to play my waltz or "God Save the King", effected an unhappy compromise by playing them both at once. The curtain fell, missing my head by a fraction. NOEL COWARD

How did the Greeks stand marble benches in their theatres?
ALDOUS HUXLEY

It is well understood by every dramatist that a late-dining audience needs several minutes of dialogue before it recovers from its bewilderment at finding itself in a theatre.
A. A. MILNE

Thence to the Theatre... Here I sitting behind in a dark place, a lady spit backwards upon me by mistake, not seeing me; but after seeing her to be a very pretty lady, I was not troubled. SAMUEL PEPYS (1633–1703)

If my readers do their fair share of the work, I daresay they will understand nearly as much of the plays *(Pleasant and Unpleasant)* as I do myself. GEORGE BERNARD SHAW

I simply do not go to the sort of plays I dislike.
GEORGE BERNARD SHAW

"Arms and the Man" was so completely misunderstood that it made my reputation as a playwright.
GEORGE BERNARD SHAW

A tired, old-fashioned, obvious thriller. The mystery is no longer who-did-it but who still wants to see it.
MILTON SHULMAN (on *The Mousetrap* – Agatha Christie)

The audience strummed their catarrhs.
ALEXANDER WOOLLCOTT

THINKING
Brain: an apparatus with which we think that we think.
AMBROSE BIERCE

The trouble with the person who always says what he thinks is that he talks more than he thinks. LAMBERT JEFFRIES

When all think alike, no one is thinking.
WALTER LIPPMANN

The captain's thoughts raced through his head like paper-bags in a hurricane. J. B. MORTON

Thinking has always been to me an occupation painful and without charm. J. J. ROUSSEAU

I have asked several men what passes through their minds when they are thinking; and I could never find any man who could think for two minutes together. SYDNEY SMITH

He could no more help having ideas about everything than a dog can resist smelling at your heels. H. G. WELLS

THOUGHTS – *see also* **PHILOSOPHY**.
One's conscience had better not speak at all than be always jabbering. SAMUEL BUTLER

Shake a hand, never a fist. A. G. ELLIOT

The good thing about swallowing pride is that it doesn't choke you. A. G. ELLIOT

There is nothing so unsatisfactory as desire satisfied.
LAMBERT JEFFRIES

The surest way of losing one's dignity is to stand on it.
LAMBERT JEFFRIES

Nothing is so firmly believed as what we least know.
MICHEL DE MONTAIGNE

To do two things at once is to do neither. PUBLILIUS SYRUS

TRAVEL – *see also* **BOATS, CARS, EXPLORATION, FLYING, IMAGINATION, MOTORING, RAILWAY, ROADS**.
Airline travel is hours of boredom interrupted by moments of stark terror. AL BOLISKA

The only times I ever knew the buses of Dublin to go fast is when I'm running to catch one. BRENDAN BEHAN

You know what it's like in a crowded bus, going through twelve pockets (for your fare), with two parcels in your teeth. J. BASIL BOOTHROYD

It's easier to find a travelling companion than to get rid of one. PEG BRACKEN

Had Cain been Scottish, God would have changed his doom: Not forced him wander, but condemned him home. JOHN CLEVELAND (1613–1658)

No harm is done as long as one understands that when a travel brochure talks about a place being "ideal to relax in" it really means that there is absolutely nothing whatever to *do*. DEREK COOPER

A toothbrush and a nightdress and a couple of little bedside books never seem to me to weigh very much. But the moment one puts them in a suitcase they become extraordinarily heavy. E. M. DELAFIELD

It's no use asking directions in the country. [You're told] that you'd better go straight down the lane, round to the right, and cross by the third stile, and keep to the left by old Johnny Melcher's cowshed, and across the seven-acre field, and through the gate by Squire Grubbins's haystack, keeping the bridle path till you come opposite the hill where the windmill used to be. J. K. JEROME

The great question about abroad is, is it worth getting there? ROSE MACAULAY

It is better to travel hopefully than to arrive, Robert Louis Stevenson assures us ... I doubt if R.L.S. ever had to sit for an hour outside Didcot station while British Rail, reluctant to admit that in winter our weather tends to be wintry, struggled to unfreeze the points. LORD MANCROFT

Nowadays you catch foreign travel rather as you caught influenza in the twenties. GEORGE MIKES

Every year one reads of motorized parties leaving London for the Far East. Some, with steaming radiators, or lack of funds, or both, get no further than the Old Kent Road. TIM SLESSOR

I love the Old Travellers ... for their witless platitudes; for their supernatural ability to bore; for their startling, their brilliant, their overwhelming mendacity. MARK TWAIN

TRUTH – *see also* FLATTERY, HONESTY, LYING.
I don't mind lies, but I hate inaccuracy. SAMUEL BUTLER

There is probably no popularly-received belief which is absolutely true. R. T. GOULD

Truth wears a different face to everybody. J. R. LOWELL

Truth is the most valuable thing we have. Let us economize it.
MARK TWAIN

Truth is never pure, and rarely simple. OSCAR WILDE

Truth is at the bottom of a bottomless well. ANON

TYPEWRITER
A typewriter has quite as much individuality as a man's handwriting. A. CONAN DOYLE

I can type /ust as well as any blessedgirl If I give my mInd to
iT. A. P. HERBERT

The typewriter, ½ike all mac&ines, has amind of it sown.
A. P. HERBERT

When I am doing a lot of typing my fingers often get quite
sore – unscrewing the top of the Tipp-Ex bottle.
LAMBERT JEFFRIES

Typewriters are either *portable*, that is, very difficult to carry,
or *non-portable,* that is, very difficult to lift. ANGELA MILNE

People who type on non-portable typewriters are nearly
always *paid,* and this means that they use all the fingers of
each hand. ANGELA MILNE

TYRANNY
Bad laws are the worst sort of tyranny. EDMUND BURKE

The best government is a benevolent tyranny, modified by an
occasional assassination. VOLTAIRE

TYRE – *see also* **FRUSTRATION.**
I know of nothing more damnably frustrating than trying to
blow up a bicycle tyre with a faulty pump.
LAMBERT JEFFRIES

UNIVERSITY – *see also* **EDUCATION, SCHOOL, TEACHERS.**

"This course of lectures," the professor told his students, "is
like a game of tennis. During the term the lecturer serves balls
to the class, and in the examination the students return balls
to the lecturer." BALAAM

No wonder, looking back, I never worked...
I cut tutorials with wild excuse,
For life was luncheons, luncheons, all the way.
JOHN BETJEMAN

Colleges hate geniuses, just as convents hate saints.
R. W. EMERSON

"Haven't you heard how they mark the tripos at Cambridge?... The old don totters back from the hall and chucks
the lot down the staircase. The ones that stick on the top flight

are given firsts. Most of them end up on the landing and get seconds." RICHARD GORDON

What distinguishes Cambridge from Oxford, broadly speaking, is that nobody who has been to Cambridge feels impelled to write about it. A. A. MILNE

"Did you sleep together?" "Only at lectures." MARK POWER

I noticed that the undergraduettes at Oxford aimed to take down every word of the lecturer, starting from "Good morning, ladies and gentlemen", and ending with "And there, I fear, we must stop for today". R. C. ROBERTSON-GLASGOW

He had hoped to open what was described as "an university for the mentally confused", but as most universities cater for these, it did not get off the ground. BYRON ROGERS

WALES – *see also* ENGLISH, FRANCE, IRISH, JEWS.
My conversation with the old man was difficult, because, although he had a perfect command of English, he chose to speak Welsh. THOMAS FIRBANK

The land of my fathers. And my fathers can have it.
DYLAN THOMAS

"From the earliest times the Welsh have been looked upon as an unclean people. It is thus that they have preserved their racial integrity." EVELYN WAUGH

"The Welsh," said the Doctor, "are the only nation in the world that has produced no graphic or plastic art... They just sing and blow down wind instruments of plated silver."
EVELYN WAUGH

I thought I was coming home when I came back to Cardiff.

But Cardiff is just a big provincial city with a lot of Welsh people in it. GWYN WILLIAMS

WALKING – *see also* COUNTRYSIDE, EXERCISE.
"Nobody walks much faster than I do."
"He can't do that," said the King, "or he'd have been here first." LEWIS CARROLL

"I nauseate walking; 'tis a country diversion."
WILLIAM CONGREVE (1670–1729)

A doctor recommended Sydney Smith to take a daily walk on an empty stomach. "Whose?" inquired Sydney. E. V. LUCAS

Almost all those who write about walking... obviously believe that there is some special merit in carrying your luggage on your back, in covering long distances, and in arriving footsore and dust-smeared at the end of the day.
ROBERT LYND

WAR – *see also* ARMY, ENEMY.
The way to win an atomic war is to make certain it never starts. GENERAL OMAR BRADLEY

Force and fraud are in war the two cardinal virtues.
THOMAS HOBBES (1588–1679)

Ben Battle was a soldier bold,
    And used to war's alarms;
But a cannon-ball took off his legs,
    So he laid down his arms. THOMAS HOOD

After the war it seemed that we would hardly survive the blow of victory; nevertheless, today we are nearly as well off as the Germans themselves. GEORGE MIKES

You can't say civilization don't advance... In every war they kill you a new way. WILL ROGERS

At my selection board interview... I told the officer I was interested in tanks. His eyes blazed with enthusiasm. "Why tanks?" he said keenly. I replied that I preferred to go into battle sitting down. PETER USTINOV

I was allowed a brief whiff of freedom before going back to school in the Army as what is so ironically, so inhumanly, so inaccurately called a Private. PETER USTINOV

WEATHER
The rain it raineth on the just,
   And also on the unjust fella;
But chiefly on the just, because
   The unjust steals the just's umbrella. C. S. BOWEN

Rain is accepted by the Londoner as an inescapable fact of life, like shaving, contraception, and Income Tax.
LEN DEIGHTON

Most things continue to function during rain, and the visitor to London is well advised to do likewise. LEN DEIGHTON

July had been blown out like a candle by a biting wind that ushered in a leaden August sky. GERALD DURRELL

Washing your car and polishing it up is a never-failing sign of rain. KIN HUBBARD

Who wants to be foretold the weather? It is bad enough when it comes, without our having the misery of knowing about it beforehand. J. K. JEROME

If December passes without snow, we indignantly demand to know what has become of our good, old-fashioned winters,

and talk as if we had been cheated out of something we had bought and paid for; and when it does snow, our language is a disgrace to a Christian nation. J. K. JEROME

We shall never be content until each man makes his own weather, and keeps it to himself. If that cannot be arranged, we would rather do without it altogether. J. K. JEROME

The rain not only fell mainly on the plain in Spain, it also fell mainly on the back of the bloody neck, dripping down the spine into the socks. SPIKE MILLIGAN

I said to the First Officer, "Gad, that sun's hot." To which he replied, "Well, you shouldn't touch it." SPIKE MILLIGAN

Rain certainly falls in Scotland (there are no recorded instances of it rising) but it also has a trick of hanging about in the air at about ear level... In the Highlands it is referred to as a "Scotch mist". FRANK MUIR

If I were running the world I would have it rain only between 2 a.m. and 5 a.m. Anyone out then ought to get wet. W. L. PHELPS

As usual, the London atmosphere has proved a complete malaria to me. The little leisure I have is employed in blowing my nose, with interludes of coughing. ROBERT SOUTHEY

"One of these days the sun will come smiling through."
"Well ... if you meet it, tell it to get a move on."
P. G. WODEHOUSE

WOMAN – *see also* BEAUTY.
A girl never pursues a man; but then, a mousetrap never pursues a mouse. RONNIE BARKER

Most women are not so young as they are painted.
MAX BEERBOHM

Even nowadays a man can't step up and kill a woman without feeling just a bit unchivalrous. ROBERT BENCHLEY

The Sunday papers are the same every week ... those ghastly obligatory articles by women on how awful it is to be a woman. JEFFREY BERNARD

Brigands demand your money or your life, whereas women require both. SAMUEL BUTLER

I have prejudices about women. I do not like to see them eat.
LORD BYRON

Up to 1945 we still retained a number of chivalrous gestures; we raised our hats to ladies, and let them pass first through doors ... And we still subscribed to the fantasy that they were chaste and pure beings. KENNETH CLARK

... trendy-looking girls who look as though they've just crawled out from underneath a rolling stone. JILLY COOPER

"What is woman? Only one of Nature's agreeable blunders."
HANNAH COWLEY

She was the sort of woman to be avoided – one who made you want to slip off her shoulder-straps but wouldn't let you.
A. G. ELLIOT

In that part of the world which is called civilized there are only three places you can avoid women – the club, the monastery, and the grave. NATHANIEL GUBBINS

Modern drugs are wonderful. They enable a wife with pneumonia to nurse her husband through 'flu.
FAITH HINES & PAM BROWN

"Women are always wonderfully the same. Shapes vary a little, that's all.' ALDOUS HUXLEY

The first conjuring trick was the production of a woman from a man's rib, but it was not very well rehearsed.
LAMBERT JEFFRIES

A woman can't be too rich, too thin, or have too many silk blouses. JOYCE JILLSON

Court a mistress, she denies you;
Let her alone, she will court you. BEN JONSON (c. 1572–1637)

The female of the species is more deadly than the male.
RUDYARD KIPLING

"Why can't a woman be more like a man?" ALAN LERNER

She's the sort of woman who lives for others – and you can
always tell the others by their hunted expression. C. S. LEWIS

Gorgeous signorine, sloe-eyed, raven-haired, pert-bosomed,
under the influence of indolence and pasta, are apt to swell
and swell. JOHN MARSHALL

Some women can't see a telephone without picking up the
receiver. W. SOMERSET MAUGHAM

Little dabs of powder,
Little smears of paint,
Make a woman's wrinkles
Look as if they ain't. HELEN MAY

God help thee (quoth the magician), for it is an easie matter to
make a woman speak, but to make her hold her tongue is past
my cunning. *Pasquil's Jests* (1604)

Women and elephants never forget an injury. SAKI

O woman in our hours of ease,
Uncertain, coy, and hard to please. WALTER SCOTT

I make it a habit, when I get restless over my work, to seize the
nearest woman and squeeze the breath out of her stays.
GEORGE BERNARD SHAW

The English woman is so refined,
She has no bosom and no behind. STEVIE SMITH

A woman with fair opportunities and without a positive hump may marry whom she likes. W. M. THACKERAY

It is one thing to be told that a tall, dark, handsome stranger is shortly to come into your life; the big trick is to nobble him. JACK THOMAS

When women go wrong, men go right after them. MAE WEST

WORK – *see also* IDLENESS.
I like work: it fascinates me. I can sit and look at it for hours. J. K. JEROME

I go on working for the same reason that a hen goes on laying eggs. H. L. MENCKEN

"He kills some six or seven Scots at breakfast, washes his hands, and says to his wife, 'Fie upon this quiet life! I want work!'" WILLIAM SHAKESPEARE *(Henry IV, Pt. I)*

There is nothing so easy but that it becomes difficult when you do it with reluctance. TERENCE (c. 195–159 B.C.)

If you want to do a thing badly, you have to work as hard at it as if you want to do it well. PETER USTINOV

WRITING – *see also* BOOKS, CRITICISM, JOURNALISM, LETTERS, POETRY, PROSE, QUOTATIONS.
A good story-teller never lets the facts get in the way. DAVE ALLEN

After you've praised a writer's last work, the conversation rather lags. W. H. AUDEN

If the tutors of correspondence courses gave discouraging

advice, their purses would grow thin, and they might themselves be driven to write for a living. BALAAM

To give an accurate and exhaustive account... would need a far less brilliant pen than mine. MAX BEERBOHM

It took me fifteen years to discover I had no talent for writing, but I couldn't give it up because by that time I was too famous. ROBERT BENCHLEY

'Tis pleasant, sure, to see one's name in print;
A book's a book, although there's nothing in't. LORD BYRON

Finishing a book is just like you took a child out in the yard and shot it. TRUMAN CAPOTE

When writers meet they do not usually talk about writing; they talk about money. PATRICK SKENE CATLING

I cannot remember one story on which I spent more than a day, and *Gamekeeper*, which you seem to like so much, I wrote in the dressing-box of an open-air swimming-bath. ANTON CHEKHOV

There are books showing men how to succeed in everything; they are written by men who cannot even succeed in writing books. G. K. CHESTERTON

He did not talk about the books he had written; he was far too much alive for that. He talked about the books he had not written. G. K. CHESTERTON

When two people are collaborating on the same book, each believes he gets all the worries and only half the royalties. AGATHA CHRISTIE

One writer I know has an unnerving habit of taking two extra copies of all his love letters, one for himself, the other for the British Museum. JILLY COOPER

"What is there in your play that you consider so deep? Apart from the plot, which is completely submerged after the first four pages." NOEL COWARD

When I want to read a book, I write one. BENJAMIN DISRAELI

This for the printer I indict:
   For every comma he puts in,
Unasked, to poems that I write,
   May he find suddenly a pin
Secreted where he lies at night,
   And may it penetrate his skin. LORD DUNSANY

My wife... pleased me by laughing uproariously when reading the manuscript, only to inform me that it was my spelling that amused her. GERALD DURRELL

Unprovided with original learning, unformed in the habits of thinking, unskilled in the arts of composition, I resolved to write a book. EDWARD GIBBON

I sit in my tiny writer's room – it's so small that even the mice are hunchbacks. KEVIN GOLDSTEIN-JACKSON

The man who is asked by an author what he thinks of his book is put to the torture, and is not obliged to speak the truth. SAMUEL JOHNSON

Sir, no man but a blockhead ever wrote except for money. SAMUEL JOHNSON

You can get rid of all your troubles by writing them down. Just put them down on paper and they vanish. W. SOMERSET MAUGHAM

The two most beautiful words in the English language are "Cheque enclosed". DOROTHY PARKER

Most great writers survive not because of their ideas but in spite of them. J. B. PRIESTLEY

When you put down the good things you ought to have done, and leave out the bad ones you did do – that's memoirs. WILL ROGERS

"The true artist will let his wife starve, his children go barefoot, his mother drudge for his living at seventy, sooner than work at anything but his art." GEORGE BERNARD SHAW

People must not be forced to adopt me as their favourite author, even for their own good. GEORGE BERNARD SHAW

If you can't write a play without being taught – don't. GEORGE BERNARD SHAW

You will never write a good book until you have written some bad ones. GEORGE BERNARD SHAW

Every successful novelist has to his name one book of which everybody says, "Why don't you write something else like *that*?" G. B. STERN

I write plays because dialogue is the most respectable way of contradicting myself. TOM STOPPARD

Three hours a day will produce as much as any man ought to write. ANTHONY TROLLOPE

Your book will not become a best-seller just because it is put on a bookstall; it is much more likely to become soiled stock. STANLEY UNWIN

The story of the creation was told in two hundred words.
Look it up if you don't believe me. EDGAR WALLACE

YOUR VOICE
How to Enrich it, and Develop it for Speaking, Acting and Everyday Conversation

A simple but valuable guide for those who want to polish and improve their most potent means of communication: the voice. Become aware of the parts of your body which need to work to peak performance for clear, dynamic and persuasive speech. Be guided through the use of crisp consonants and well shaped vowels. Learn expressiveness, projection, confidence and relaxation.

THE RIGHT WAY TO
CONDUCT MEETINGS

This book is for the Chairmen of voluntary organisations, and for all those who want to understand procedure in Councils, debating, etc.

It explains the pivotal role of the Chairman in getting the business completed quickly, efficiently, and without loss of humour. It covers procedure for meetings, conferences and discussions of all kinds. Special attention is given to motions, amendments and resolutions.

PRESENTATIONS
The Right Way To Make Effective Presentations

The author has given hundreds of presentations all over the world, both for sales and technical purposes, and for training. This book is derived from a training course which he has developed for a multinational conglomerate with over 100,000 employees.

BRUSH UP YOUR GRAMMAR

Brush Up Your Grammar helps readers to understand grammatical terms, chapter by chapter, in a way that increases self-confidence and builds on previous knowledge. It avoids jargon and is addressed to those who may be intimidated by the complexity of formal grammar. It is a book which will encourage you to look more closely at language in a stimulating and enjoyable way.

QUIRKY QUIZ QUESTIONS

Searching for an oddball quiz? This book turns your everyday quiz question on its head, with its cheeky twists on theme, and with its puns making any quiz time more entertaining. The author brings to his quiz a particular brand of style and humour that covers a range of subjects within one theme. A quiz book for the discerning "idiosyncrat".

READY-MADE QUIZZES

A unique book of ready-made quizzes. All the quizzes are designed to be used straight from the book. For easy reference, each answer appears either on the same page as the question or is given overleaf. Although this popular book was designed for use by quiz masters, it has become a hit with all quiz enthusiasts. It isn't just for quiz organisers and participants; it will also provide hours of fun for families and all who enjoy testing their own general knowledge.

THE PUBLIC SPEAKER'S
JOKE BOOK

With its easy-to-follow Joke Directory and with the jokes arranged by subject, this is the ideal book for the public speaker (or for a hilarious read on a plane or train journey or for a chuckle in bed). The collection contains over 500 jokes with will suit every occasion: business functions, conventions, dinners, weddings and children's parties, so you'll never be lost for a humorous quip.

THE RIGHT JOKE FOR THE
RIGHT OCCASION

Everyone can reduce their friends to helpless peals of laughter with this joke book. Locate your joke either by consulting the unique subject suitability list, or by making use of the A-Z sequence of the book. Whether you are searching for a joke about artificial insemination, the birds and the bees, or about camels, cars or cats, you should find it here.

SAMPLE SOCIAL SPEECHES

This book includes sample speeches for every social occasion. There's also information on how to prepare and deliver a speech, as well as lots of anecdotes, aphorisms and stories for you to include in your speech.

BEST MAN'S DUTIES

The best man is certainly the third most important person at any wedding ceremony. This book is the ideal detailed guide for this special person. It includes everything from his duties at the bridegroom's stag party to his role at the service and reception, as well as a sample speech.

WEDDING ETIQUETTE PROPERLY EXPLAINED

An invaluable handbook which covers everything the bride and groom need to know when preparing for their wedding: the legal requirements, the banns, the details of the church service, planning the reception, the catering arrangements, plus much more.

WEDDING SPEECHES

This book consists entirely of wedding speeches. Every one is different, amusing, to the point and lively. Any of them can easily be adapted to particular circumstances, or delivered as it stands.

There are 15 speeches for the bridegroom, 15 for the best man, 12 for the bride's father (along with another 8 suitable for occasions when the bride's father does not speak), and 15 which are suitable for other relations and friends who may want to say something.

RIGHT WAY
PUBLISHING POLICY

HOW WE SELECT TITLES

RIGHT WAY consider carefully every deserving manuscript. Where an author is an authority on his subject but an inexperienced writer, we provide first-class editorial help. The standards we set make sure that every **RIGHT WAY** book is practical, easy to understand, concise, informative and delightful to read. Our specialist artists are skilled at creating simple illustrations which augment the text wherever necessary.

CONSISTENT QUALITY

At every reprint our books are updated where appropriate, giving our authors the opportunity to include new information.

FAST DELIVERY

We sell **RIGHT WAY** books to the best bookshops throughout the world. It may be that your bookseller has run out of stock of a particular title. If so, he can order more from us at any time – we have a fine reputation for "same day" despatch, and we supply any order, however small (even a single copy), to any bookseller who has an account with us. We prefer you to buy from your bookseller, as this reminds him of the strong underlying public demand for **RIGHT WAY** books. Readers who live in remote places, or who are housebound, or whose local bookseller is uncooperative, can order direct from us by post.

FREE

If you would like an up-to-date list of all **RIGHT WAY** titles currently available, please send a stamped self-addressed envelope to ELLIOT RIGHT WAY BOOKS, BRIGHTON ROAD,
LOWER KINGSWOOD, TADWORTH, SURREY, KT20 6TD, U.K.
or visit our web site at www.right-way.co.uk